NEW DIRECTIONS FOR TEACHING AND LEARNING

Marilla D. Svinicki, *University of Texas, Austin*
EDITOR-IN-CHIEF

R. Eugene Rice, *American Association for Higher Education*
CONSULTING EDITOR

Scholarship in the Postmodern Era: New Venues, New Values, New Visions

Kenneth J. Zahorski
St. Norbert College

EDITOR

Number 90, Summer 2002

JOSSEY-BASS
San Francisco

SCHOLARSHIP IN THE POSTMODERN ERA: NEW VENUES, NEW VALUES, NEW VISIONS
Kenneth J. Zahorski (ed.)
New Directions for Teaching and Learning, no. 90
Marilla D. Svinicki, Editor-in-Chief
R. Eugene Rice, Consulting Editor

Microfilm copies of issues and articles are available in 16mm and 35mm, as well as microfiche in 105mm, through University Microfilms Inc., 300 North Zeeb Road, Ann Arbor, Michigan 48106-1346.

ISSN 0271-0633   electronic ISSN 1536-0768   ISBN 0-7879-6293-7

NEW DIRECTIONS FOR TEACHING AND LEARNING is part of The Jossey-Bass Higher and Adult Education Series and is published quarterly by Wiley Subscription Services, Inc., a Wiley company, at Jossey-Bass, 989 Market Street, San Francisco, California 94103-1741. Periodicals postage paid at San Francisco, California, and at additional mailing offices. Postmaster: Send address changes to New Directions for Teaching and Learning, Jossey-Bass, 989 Market Street, San Francisco, California 94103-1741.

New Directions for Teaching and Learning is indexed in College Student Personnel Abstracts, Contents Pages in Education, and Current Index to Journals in Education (ERIC).

SUBSCRIPTIONS cost $65.00 for individuals and $130 for institutions, agencies, and libraries. Prices subject to change.

EDITORIAL CORRESPONDENCE should be sent to the editor-in-chief, Marilla D. Svinicki, The Center for Teaching Effectiveness, University of Texas at Austin, Main Building 2200, Austin, TX 78712-1111.

Cover photograph by Richard Blair/Color & Light © 1990.

www.josseybass.com

Printed in the United States of America on acid-free recycled paper containing at least 20 percent postconsumer wase.

CONTENTS

About This Publication. Since 1980, *New Directions for Teaching and Learning (NDTL)* has brought a unique blend of theory, research, and practice to leaders in postsecondary education. *NDTL* sourcebooks strive not only for solid substance but also for timeliness, compactness, and accessibility.

The series has four goals: to inform readers about current and future directions in teaching and learning in postsecondary education, to illuminate the context that shapes these new directions, to illustrate these new directions through examples from real settings, and to propose ways in which these new directions can be incorporated into still other settings.

This publication reflects the view that teaching deserves respect as a high form of scholarship. We believe that significant scholarship is conducted not only by researchers who report results of empirical investigations but also by practitioners who share disciplines' reflections about teaching. Contributors to *NDTL* approach questions of teaching and learning as seriously as they approach substantive questions in their own disciplines, and they deal not only with pedagogical issues but also with the intellectual and social context in which these issues arise. Authors deal on the one hand with theory and research and on the other with practice, and they translate from research and theory to practice and back again.

About This Volume. In this issue, the authors ask questions about how faculty notions of scholarship have changed in the wake of Boyer's *Scholarship Reconsidered* (1990), how institutions are changing their promotion and tenure policies, and the way they conduct the business of fostering faculty scholarship. The authors offer both theory and practice to address new ways of thinking about faculty work and lives.

Marilla D. Svinicki
Editor-in-Chief

MARILLA D. SVINICKI *is director of the Center for Teaching Effectiveness at the University of Texas at Austin.*

EDITOR'S NOTES

The twin peaks of teaching and scholarship rise above all other highlands in academe's vast domain. But although both promontories are duly admired and respected, only upon one have educators regularly lavished their critical attention. Teaching is often the subject of academic discourse; scholarship, though, has been largely ignored as a subject of critical exploration, treated for the most part like a frequently passed landmark too familiar to warrant comment. All this changed, however, in 1990, when Ernest Boyer's *Scholarship Reconsidered* (1990) burst onto the scene, igniting an energetic national conversation that maintains its vitality to this day. Our intent is to enter, and enrich, that conversation. Five tenets form this issue's philosophic infrastructure.

First, this issue aims at covering new territory, at taking a different slant on the topic of scholarship. Of course, readers will still find here discussed some of the most familiar (and key) issues in the national debate—issues ranging from strategies for promoting, nurturing, and supporting scholarship to methods for evaluating and rewarding it. However, every effort has been made to use these oft-visited sites as launching pads for fresh exploration. Our guiding principle, then, has been to take a step, or two, beyond familiar terrain.

Second, and closely related to the first tenet, contributors have not only been invited but have also been urged to take risks, to, in the best tradition of *Star Trek*, "boldly go where no [one] has gone before." Glassick, Huber, and Maeroff (1997) identify "courage" as one of the three most important attributes of the scholar, explaining that a "scholar must have the courage to risk disapproval in the name of candor" (p. 65). This issue's contributors have accepted that risk, treating sensitive, sometimes controversial, issues with boldness and honesty. In short, we have tried not to shy away from volatile issues, recognizing that vexing problems, if they are to be solved, must be confronted head on.

Third, this issue is future-oriented. The beginning of a new century is a time not only for reflection and retrospection but also for speculation and conjecture; a time not only for taking stock of where we have been and what has resulted from that journey but also for looking ahead and preparing to meet the challenges of future journeys. In an age of exponential change, perhaps our greatest hope for harnessing and exploiting this change is to extrapolate well and wisely enough to practice foresight rather than nonreflective reaction. One of the primary goals of this issue, then, is to get a fix on scholarship's future direction. More specifically, the volume attempts to assess the catalytic effect *Scholarship Reconsidered* has had on the attitudes toward, and practices of, scholarship at the beginning of the new millennium.

Fourth, this issue moves beyond institutional concerns to the concerns of the individual, beyond the theoretical to the practical. We try to bring scholarship issues down to a workaday level. For example, how has *Scholarship Reconsidered* measurably influenced, on a day-to-day basis, the professional and personal lives of teacher-scholars? How has the technology revolution changed the way we do scholarship? How do departmental and institutional expectations, as manifested in scholarship policies, affect our quest for personal and professional fulfillment? These are big questions in need of equally substantive answers.

Fifth, this issue is driven by the foundational assumption that although academe has made some progress in humanizing the policies governing scholarship, even more humane, equitable, and compassionate policies and practices are needed. We must continue to strive for a potent repertoire of strategies for transforming the scholarly endeavor from an activity that stresses and exhausts its practitioners into one that renews, reenergizes, and rejuvenates them, ultimately bringing happiness, enrichment, and satisfaction. We must continue to seek ways of achieving balance in our professional and personal lives, a balance leading toward renewal rather than burnout, toward fulfillment rather than frustration.

This issue's structure reflects and honors these five foundational tenets. The first three chapters share the theme of New Venues, focusing on the new settings, the new circumstances, the new cultural environments in which the act of scholarship is now being, and will be, played out. In Chapter One, R. Eugene Rice sets the stage by providing not only a retrospective analysis of the influence of *Scholarship Reconsidered* but also a critique of the changes this influential Carnegie report has produced, ending with a commentary on what we can expect, as well as what we need next, within the realm of scholarship. This framing chapter, written by one of the key players in the move toward a broader definition of scholarship, builds the context needed to bring full meaning to the ensuing chapters. Wallace Hannum, in Chapter Two, follows up with a discerning look at the powerful influence of computers and information technology on the scholarly process, providing the reader with concrete evidence of how computer technology has influenced most aspects of scholarship, from formulating ideas and gathering data to collaborating and publishing research results. Indeed, Hannum concludes that because of computer technology we are now witnessing a "dramatic transformation in both the process and power of scholarship." In Chapter Three, Kenneth Zahorski argues that the key requisite for scholarship is an institution-wide culture of hope and opportunity. Drawing from nearly two decades of experience as director of a holistic faculty development program, Zahorski describes a strategy for creating a nurturing environment for scholarship, he then discusses some of the intrainstitutional partnerships that promote scholarly endeavors, and finally, he lists a few of the benefits derived from this holistic strategy.

This issue's middle three chapters, coming under the rubric of New Values, identify and explore the fresh set of values currently informing, or on the brink of informing, today's scholarly practices. In Chapter Four, Mary Deane Sorcinelli begins the conversation with an important reminder of how tenure review policies and practices profoundly affect the scholarly endeavor. Only when we make the tenure process more effective, flexible, and humane, says Sorcinelli, will we succeed in validating and encouraging the multiple types of scholarship proposed in *Scholarship Reconsidered*. Although the task ahead is truly challenging, admits Sorcinelli, significant progress has already been made, and the future offers us a "wonderful opportunity" not only to enhance our approach to scholarship but also to "further transform our conceptions of faculty work and of the academy itself." Anne F. Lucas, in Chapter Five, celebrates the department as the standard bearer of organizational units possessing the power to help faculty members become productive, happy scholars. And just how can the department become a key player in promoting scholarship? Transform the unit into a cohesive team built on a foundation of trust, urges Lucas. Only through a departmental climate that is "humanitarian and supportive" can one hope to significantly increase scholarly productivity. Recognizing that department chairs are central to the transformation process, Lucas provides the reader with a valuable list of specific interventions that chairs can employ to generate change in departmental cultures. In Chapter Six, Kina Mallard rounds off the thesis of New Values with a clarion call for a paradigm shift in the way institutions view, promote, nurture, and reward scholarship—a fresh and holistic approach that focuses not so much on the scholarly product as on the well-being of the scholarly practitioner. She issues a challenge to college and university leaders to consider "scholar-development stages" and to develop "scholar-mentoring programs," with the goal of developing a "community of dialogue."

The final three chapters, concerned with New Visions, look to the future of scholarship, identifying trends, causative factors, and potentialities that promise to shape scholars and their scholarship in the new millennium. In Chapter Seven, Robert Diamond leads off with an insightful discussion that identifies primary influences upon scholarship, recent developments in how we view the scholarly role of faculty members, and an institutional approach for bringing fairness and quality into faculty renewal systems. Grounding his commentary in large part on the extensive and pioneering work he has done with disciplinary association task forces, Diamond suggests that the future of scholarship will be considerably brighter if we "focus more on the qualities that make an activity scholarly and less on the specific activity itself." Ronald Dotterer, in Chapter Eight, envisions an equally bright and dynamic future for scholarship if we replace the archetype of the scholar working in isolation with the collaborative investigative model. Especially promising, writes Dotterer, is collaborative inquiry-based education. Collaboration, involving either student-faculty or administrative-faculty interactions, "offers an exciting and effective new heuristic." And, finally, in Chapter Nine, Jerry Berberet envisions a new era of scholarship built on the firm foundation of community engagement. Using the New

American College institutional model as a source of inspiration, instruction, and guidance, Berberet convincingly argues that "the idea of moving from modernism to a postmodern era, although simplistic, involves a paradigm shift for which a scholarship of community engagement is a logical expression." However, he continues, if the scholarship of community engagement is to blossom, we must develop new epistemologies, and "constructing an epistemology for the scholarship of community engagement requires both the rethinking of the nature and purposes of scholarship that Boyer initiated and assumptions about truth and ground rules for determining it that are consistent with the emerging paradigms of the postmodern era."

Perhaps the grandest of legacies of the national conversation generated by *Scholarship Reconsidered* would be the creation of a "gentler and kinder" approach to promoting, evaluating, and rewarding scholarship: an approach emphasizing nurturance, inclusivity, enlightened assessment, and an equitable reward system. I hope that in some small way this issue helps ensure that legacy.

Kenneth J. Zahorski
Editor

References

Boyer, E. L. *Scholarship Reconsidered: Priorities of the Professoriate.* Menlo Park, Calif.: Carnegie Foundation for the Advancement of Teaching, 1990.

Glassick, C. E., Huber, M. T., and Maeroff, G. I. *Scholarship Assessed: Evaluation of the Professoriate.* San Francisco: Jossey-Bass, 1997.

KENNETH J. ZAHORSKI is professor of English and director of faculty development at St. Norbert College, De Pere, Wisconsin.

PART ONE

New Venues

Ernest Boyer's 1990 Carnegie report, Scholarship Reconsidered, *is examined as a "tipping point"—a critical turning point in what is fundamentally valued and rewarded in the scholarly work of faculty members. Special attention is given to the scholarship of teaching and the scholarship of engagement.*

Beyond *Scholarship Reconsidered:* Toward an Enlarged Vision of the Scholarly Work of Faculty Members

R. Eugene Rice

In the late 1980s serious questions were being raised about how faculty members use their time. Legislators and trustees—even those who had genuinely befriended higher education—were deeply concerned about the quality of undergraduate teaching. Increasingly, the scholarship of most professors was seen as too narrowly specialized and self-referential. In airport bookstores, popular diatribes such as Charles J. Sykes's *ProfScam* (1988) were readily available. On campuses, the old teaching versus research debate raged on ad nauseam. Faculty scholarship was regarded by all too many as fundamentally disconnected from the larger purposes of American society.

By the end of the decade, Derek Bok (1990) would render this stinging indictment:

> Armed with the security of tenure and the time to study the world with care, professors would appear to have a unique opportunity to act as society scouts to signal impending problems long before they are visible to others. Yet rarely have members of the academy succeeded in discovering the emerging issues and bringing them vividly to the attention of the public. What Rachael Carson did for risks to the environment, Ralph Nader for consumer protection, Michael Harrington for problems of poverty, Betty Friedan for women's rights, they did as independent critics, not as members of the faculty. Even the seminal work on the plight of blacks in America was written by a Swedish social scientist, not a member of an American university.
>
> After a major social problem has been recognized, universities will usually continue to respond weakly unless outside support is available and the

subjects involved command prestige in academic circles. These limitations have hampered efforts to address many of the most critical challenges to the nation [p. 105].

This was the environment and the set of concerns that gave rise to Ernest Boyer's 1990 Carnegie report.

Scholarship Reconsidered—A "Tipping Point"

More than to review the legacy of *Scholarship Reconsidered* or to celebrate its impact over the past decade, the intent of this chapter is to view the Carnegie report as a "tipping point" phenomenon—a critical turning point in what is fundamentally valued in the scholarly work of faculty members. Malcolm Gladwell's new book, *The Tipping Point* (2000), helps us understand the organizational change process. *Scholarship Reconsidered* was a brief, to-the-point document of less than sixty pages that told us little that we did not already know. However, it did come along at the right time and it addressed the major strains that had developed around the scholarship issue. Most important, it reframed the issue, so that we could get beyond the old teaching versus research debate, rise above the theory/practice hierarchy plaguing higher education, and begin to think in new ways about the alignment of faculty priorities and institutional mission.

In reframing the discussion of what is valued as scholarly work, *Scholarship Reconsidered* may have served as a "tipping point" in the closing decade of the twentieth century, much as was the case with another Carnegie report, *The Flexner Report* (Flexner, 1910), in the opening years of the century. Abraham Flexner's 1910 report on medical education transformed the whole approach to professional education. Schools of medicine were moved into research universities and the scientific component of medical education was markedly increased. Theory and research were given precedence over clinical practice. The 1910 Carnegie report came along at precisely the right time—tipping the balance—and setting in place the hierarchical structure of the key components of professional knowledge for much of the rest of the century. As the other professional fields developed, they adopted the Flexner priorities and followed medicine's suit.

Whether *Scholarship Reconsidered* will have the kind of pivotal influence exhibited by the earlier Carnegie report (Flexner, 1910) will not be fully evident for years to come. It did come along at a very propitious moment, was advocated by a key leader in educational reform at the height of his career, was formulated in response to substantial currents of social and political discontent, and drew on intellectual resources that were circulating around various sectors of higher education but had not been drawn together in a coherent way and focused on the scholarly work of faculty members.

Because I was involved in the formulation of *Scholarship Reconsidered* and later directed a national project committed to its implementation, I have been asked to give my personal assessment of the changes that have taken place in the way we think about and value the scholarly work of faculty members since the publication of the report. I was at the Carnegie Foundation for the Advancement of Teaching from 1988 to 1990, when the ideas that went into *Scholarship Reconsidered* were being developed. Following a stint as dean of the faculty and vice president at Antioch College, I moved to Washington, D.C., and I now direct the American Association for Higher Education's Forum on Faculty Roles and Rewards. My perspective on this topic was profoundly shaped by my direct involvement in the original development of, and then my efforts to implement, the Carnegie report on scholarship. It is a biased perspective that is, I hope, marked by greater clarity because of that direct engagement. This reflects an epistemological assumption that is endemic to the entire report and the work it has stimulated over the past ten years.

In looking at *Scholarship Reconsidered* as a "tipping point," it needs to be made clear that the 1990 Carnegie report was intended from the beginning to be heuristic. It was never intended to impose a particular formulation of the scholarly work of faculty members on American higher education. The report's primary purpose was to reframe the discussion and to open a lively conversation across campuses and disciplines about what faculty members do as scholars on a broad range of fronts. *Scholarship Reconsidered* was a search for new ideas and fresh conceptions of faculty work that would reunite personal and institutional endeavors, bring wholeness to scholarly lives, and, at the same time, meet the broadly diverse and changing educational needs of society.

Scholarship Reconsidered obviously struck a responsive chord. The monograph very quickly became the best-selling publication in the history of the Carnegie Foundation. Colleges and universities across the nation, and across sectors, began to reexamine their tenure and promotion guidelines. Substantive questions about the relationship between faculty priorities and institutional mission began to be raised in a new way.

Ernest Boyer's leadership was pivotal in advancing the reexamination of the faculty role and the reward structure, with special focus on the work of the scholar. No one else had the eloquence, persuasiveness, national visibility, and, frankly, the audacity to take on the task of redefining scholarship. He combined charismatic authority with positional authority in a way that is almost unique in recent American higher education. Furthermore, his insistence that the Carnegie Foundation "speak with one voice" gave the ideas generated out of the institution unusual force. Boyer also brought from his years of political experience in Washington, D.C., and Albany an uncanny sense of timing; nowhere was this talent more fully evident than in the development and release of his 1990 report on faculty scholarship. Following the publication of *Scholarship Reconsidered,* Boyer committed his very active speaking schedule and writing to the dissemination of the broader notion of scholarship set forth in the report. I have been on more than one university campus where rather heavy-handed provosts and deans were imposing the definitions of scholarship articulated in *Scholarship Reconsidered* and found resistant faculty members complaining of being "Boyerized."

Moving to the Heart of the Academic Enterprise

Most reports calling for change in higher education—from foundations, associations, and various think tanks—inspire an initial flurry of activity and then disappear. This was not the case with *Scholarship Reconsidered,* in part because the report articulated concerns already visible in the educational climate and drew together ideas ripe for wider attention. To ensure that the broader conception of scholarship set forth in the 1990 Carnegie report would not disappear, however, a new organizational initiative was put into place. Russell Edgerton led the American Association for Higher Education (AAHE) (with major support from the Fund for the Improvement of Post-Secondary Education) in establishing the AAHE's Forum on Faculty Roles and Rewards. In his keynote address at one of the early annual conferences of the Forum, Ernest Boyer (1990a) described how "we are beginning to find a new language, a common language. . . . that will help revitalize research, give dignity to teaching, and help the academy be more responsive."

Of the many influences supporting the reconsideration of scholarship, none has been more important than the involvement of the various academic disciplines and their professional associations. Those familiar with academic culture know that most faculty members have their identities imbedded in their disciplines and align themselves institutionally with their departments. It was clear early on that any effort to enlarge the conception of scholarly work would have to recognize the disciplinary context within which scholarship is enacted and would need to bring the disciplines into the process of reconsideration. Thanks to the leadership of Robert Diamond and his colleagues at Syracuse University, the professional and disciplinary associations became actively involved in developing guidelines for evaluating and rewarding a broader conception of the scholarly work of faculty members. Professors in the disciplines struggled with the language being used and its relation to the specific field of inquiry. The arts, as might be expected, had the most difficulty with terminology, but they addressed problems—some for the first time—confounding tenure and promotion committees across higher education.

The result of this work with the disciplines is available in two volumes edited by Robert Diamond and Bronwyn Adam (1995, 2000). In these two books are the statements of twenty professional and disciplinary associations, completed after long and involved debates across the disciplinary member-ship and their representative boards. In going to the associations where faculty members have their scholarly identities, this national project advanced the discussion of what counts as scholarship in the tenure process and gave it a legitimacy it would not have had otherwise.

In contrast to most reform initiatives in higher education, where the main thrust of the change effort stays on the periphery of the college or university and gets marginalized, *Scholarship Reconsidered* took the debate to the heart of the academic enterprise—to the definitions of scholarship and to what faculty members are rewarded for doing. Moving the debate on to the disciplines and the departments reinforced its centrality. Over the past decade, it is in the disciplines and the departments that some of the liveliest discussions have ensued and the greatest gains have been made.

AAHE's 2000 Conference on Faculty Roles and Rewards marked the tenth anniversary of the publication of *Scholarship Reconsidered* (Boyer, 1990b) and took as its central theme "*Scholarship Reconsidered* Reconsidered: Up-date and New Directions." It was organized around the four forms of scholarship and their interrelationship: the scholarship of teaching, engagement, integration, and discovery. In looking at the new work that has been unleashed since the publication of the 1990 Carnegie report, I want to turn first to the form of scholarly work where the largest advances have been made in the last ten years—the scholarship of teaching. This chapter concludes by examining briefly the "scholarship of engagement"—a form of scholarly work now generating a major upsurge of interest and serious reconceptualization.

The Scholarship of Teaching

When the conceptual framework for *Scholarship Reconsidered* was being constructed, there was already a group of distinguished scholars devoting their professional lives to what later took on the designation "scholarship of teaching." The names William Perry, Joseph Katz, and Lee Shulman stand out. Firm intellectual foundations had been laid for acknowledging teaching as a scholarly enterprise. Without their preparatory contribution, the "tipping point" I have been writing about would not have been reached; the work that is now being conducted under the rubric "scholarship of teaching" would not have moved forward. Their work challenged a number of the terms being considered: the presentation of knowledge was one, and the transmission and dissemination of knowledge were also discussed. All were found to be too one-sided, and did not encompass the interactive character of this aspect of scholarship. They also reinforced the misperception that teaching is merely a packaging and distribution function. All three suggest that teaching and learning stand in a hierarchical relationship. Knowledge is viewed as a finished product; ideas are refined and then passed "down."

Lee Shulman, in a seminal essay "Knowledge and Teaching: Foundations of the New Reform" (1987), reminded us that teaching is a much more dynamic endeavor, transcending the content/process, theory/practice, teacher/student dichotomies that usually shape our thinking. He introduced the awkward but useful term "pedagogical content knowledge" into the conversation. Shulman and his colleagues worked with faculty members in specific disciplines and discovered that there is a knowledge base that is required for effective teaching that is content-specific. It is, in his words, "the capacity of a teacher to transform the content knowledge he or she possesses into forms that are pedagogically powerful and yet adaptive to the variations in an ability and background presented by the students" (p. 5).

In addition to new ways of thinking about teaching and scholarship, there were national projects that, in a practical way, moved the agenda forward. One initiative that proved to be especially pivotal was the AAHE's peer review of teaching project. Campuses worked together to create new roles for faculty members in improving and ensuring the quality of teaching and learning. Most of the work was organized around disciplines and specific scholarly societies. As with research, where there is a community of discourse and scholarly work is openly shared, critiqued, and evaluated, institutions and disciplines are now beginning to make teaching a public, documented endeavor. Faculty members in specific disciplines work together to develop strategies for reviewing and documenting the intellectual quality of the teaching and whether students are learning what is intended. The participating campuses in the peer review project were for the most part large research universities—for instance, the University of Michigan and Northwestern University. Other institutions with a reputation for taking teaching seriously, such as Alverno College and Xavier University of Louisiana, were included. The peer review of teaching project began with prestigious institutions and faculty leaders with traditional scholarly credentials already intact. As a change strategy, this was intentional.

No longer does the peer review of teaching depend chiefly on the impression of a department chair, the anecdotes of a member of the tenure committee, or one report of a classroom observation. Teaching as scholarly inquiry becomes subject to empirical evidence and the focus of collaborative intellectual inquiry. The peer review of teaching projects generated a wide range of challenging strategies that soon began to be identified as elements of the scholarship of teaching.

Included in the initiatives generated out of the peer review project were teaching circles started at the University of Nebraska, Lincoln, and patterned after Japanese quality circles. At the University of Georgia, similar groups meet to grapple with teaching large classes. At Rio Hondo College, faculty members collaborate about teaching on-line and assessing student learning. A teaching circle at Portland State University led the way in developing portfolios for promotion and tenure decisions. Peter Seldin (1997) reports that as many as a thousand colleges and universities are now using portfolios to provide a fuller assessment of teaching for personnel decision making.

Critical to the establishment and ongoing vitality of the scholarship of teaching was the appointment of Lee Shulman as president of the Carnegie Foundation for the Advancement of Teaching, following the passing of Ernest Boyer. Shulman had provided the intellectual underpinnings for AAHE's peer review of teaching project. In his new position, Shulman established the Carnegie Academy for the Scholarship of Teaching and Learning (CASTL) and the Carnegie Scholars program. CASTL is a national network of institutions with teaching academies. This program now has over two hundred colleges and universities wrestling with what the scholarship of teaching and learning means for their campuses. These institutions range from Brown University to Augustana College and from Middlesex Community College to the University of Minnesota. Disciplinary associations are also included in this national initiative. At their annual meetings, the Academy of Management, the American Chemical Society, and the American Sociological Association sponsor symposia on the scholarship of teaching.

As part of a broader view of the scholarly work of faculty members, teaching can be seen as an intellectually challenging task that transcends the exaggerated dichotomies between content and process and between research and teaching. Teaching and learning are emerging as sources of rich, scholarly discourse that have the potential to become the basis for intrinsically rewarding associations and cosmopolitan, public exchange, and they can also be evaluated and assessed with increasing confidence.

The Scholarship of Engagement

Whereas the scholarship of teaching is commanding increased attention and undergraduate teaching has been elevated in the faculty rewards process in many colleges and universities, another form of scholarly work is gaining strength—some would say, renewing its place—as an essential ingredient of scholarship. The scholarship of engagement, as it is now being conceptualized, calls for a major epistemological challenge to the more traditional view of the scholarly work of faculty members and the dominant way knowledge is generated in the academy. The discussion of engaged scholarship today is moving even beyond what was called "the scholarship of application" a decade ago in *Scholarship Reconsidered.* Although honoring what can be learned from practice, the scholarship of application assumes that the established epistemology—where knowledge is generated by faculty members in the university and then applied in external contexts— remains undisturbed and unchallenged. The scholarship of engagement requires going beyond the "expert" model that both informs and gets in the way of constructive university-community collaboration.

The scholarship of engagement being advanced now builds on the important work done by Ernest Lynton (1995) and Lynton and Driscoll (1999). These contributions have advanced our ability to document and promote recognition for faculty work in the application of knowledge. We are now prepared, however, to move beyond those endeavors in fundamental ways. In articulating the scholarship of engagement, faculty members committed to this work are not just calling for "outreach," as has been the case with the land-grant universities with their agricultural roots. Nor do they want to settle for "service," with its overtones of noblesse oblige. Rather, what is being emphasized is *collaboration*. The learning and instruction will be multidirectional and the expertise will be shared. This represents a basic reconceptualization of faculty involvement in community-based work and will require a concerted effort across disciplines and institutional sectors. It will also involve bringing community representatives into the planning and discussion at the beginning.

Thinking about the scholarship of engagement has benefited enormously from the substantive work of the late Donald Schon (1983) on "the reflective practitioner." He was an active leader in the reconsideration of scholarship, and his argument that "the new scholarship requires a new epistemology" (1995, p. 27) continues to be very influential. Schon persuasively argued that theory and research, on the one hand, and practice, on the other, had to be realigned, and that in the dominant view of faculty scholarship, theory and practice are hierarchically related, with practice being considered secondary and derivative. He then went on to contend that universities develop an "institutional epistemology" and that "they hold conceptions of what counts as legitimate knowledge and how you know what you claim to know" (1995, p. 34). These theories of knowledge are built into institutional structures and practices—most tellingly in the faculty reward system.

The most recent work on the scholarship of engagement has three components, which parallels the three traditional elements in faculty work: teaching, research, and service. They are engaged pedagogy, community-based research, and collaborative practice.

Engaged Pedagogy. The pedagogical dimensions of the scholarship of engagement require a radically different approach to teaching and learning. If effective learning in such engaged pedagogies as service-learning and learning communities is contextual and social, and if they involve experiencing what it means to be a community—as is claimed—faculty members have to rethink their relationship to students and many of their fundamental assumptions about teaching.

Community-Based Research. In community-based research, the scholarship of engagement calls for a realignment of local and cosmopolitan knowledge. Pure research that is objective, abstract, and analytical is most highly valued and has legitimacy because it can be peer-reviewed by cosmopolitan colleagues, independent of place. Community-based research is of necessity local—rooted in a particular time and setting. The most knowledgeable peers might well be representatives of the local community and not of the academy. Community-based research calls for shared expertise and challenges established academic criteria. It also needs to be collaborative and requires that the learning be multidirectional, not university-centered and campus-bound.

The profound need—and case—for university-community collaboration has been forcefully articulated by Mary Walshok (1995). There are faculty members across the country and across disciplines who are deeply committed to community-based research and who see the need for engagement as researchers in the larger community but feel restrained by the dominant view of what counts as legitimate scholarship. Nowhere is the clear articulation and support of the scholarship of engagement more urgently needed.

At a time when communities are challenged to improve their capabilities, and colleges and universities must demonstrate their public accountability, community-based research is a way to both strengthen community capacity and respond to the civic responsibility of our institutions of higher education. In contrast with past community research practice, in which community members were simply "human subjects" and passive recipients of information, community-based research—or participatory action research, as it is sometimes called—values the local community perspective and brings it into every phase of the research process.

Collaborative Practice. Work on the third component of the scholarship of engagement begins by taking seriously what Ira Harkavy at the University of Pennsylvania and others have called the Noah Principle: "No more prizes for predicting rain. Prizes only for building the arks." The focus here is on concrete, protracted community-based problems. Harkavy and his colleagues at the University of Pennsylvania have modeled the kind of local, problem-centered collaborative practice being discussed here in their work with the community issues and public schools in West Philadelphia (the geographic community located adjacent to the University). The strategy being employed here and replicated elsewhere connects school and school system change to a process of democratic community change and development. The strategy is directed at "taping, integrating, mobilizing, and galvanizing the enormous untapped, unintegrated resources of communities, including colleges and universities, to improve schooling and community life" (Benson and Harkavy, forthcoming, p. 2).

The community-higher education-school partnerships, like the ones being developed in West Philadelphia, are the kinds of collaborative practice that are desperately needed. Similar efforts to respond to pressing social needs can be found in local efforts to sustain healthy communities, maintain adequate housing, and combat prejudice. A major stumbling block to active college and university participation in this sort of collaborative work, however, is our inability to attract faculty members who see engagement of this kind as scholarly work that is legitimate, supported, and rewarded.

The scholarship of teaching and learning as part of an enlarged vision of the scholarly work of faculty members has established a firm foothold in the faculty reward systems of many colleges and universities. The scholarship of engagement is only beginning to make a coherent case for recognition that is more than local and idiosyncratic.

"Tipping Point" or "Overloaded Plate"

Reflections on the future of faculty work—and, in this volume, the impact of *Scholarship Reconsidered*—are filled with analogies. I have suggested one: a "tipping point." Another analogy that has emerged from extensive interviews with early-career faculty members is an "overloaded plate" (Rice, Sorcinelli, and Austin, 2000). The first suggests progress, a significant advance; the second, a dire warning. The new faculty members we interviewed reported that, in one sense, it is a new day on campus. Many noted that excellence in teaching is not only expected but is also beginning to be acknowledged and rewarded. Some, though many fewer, see scholarly engagement gaining ground. This is happening, while, at the same time, research and publication retain their dominance in the reward system. There is evidence that what counts as scholarly work is expanding.

An implicit change strategy—an incremental, add-on approach—has been implemented. The scholarly responsibilities of early-career faculty members have not only broadened but have also increased. As our conception of scholarly excellence has become multidimensional, what new faculty members are being held accountable for has enlarged. *Scholarship Reconsidered* has become one of a number of change initiatives escalating what is required for faculty advancement in most colleges and universities. Interviews with new faculty members identified this as a serious problem that must be addressed if we want to attract the best of a new generation into the academic profession. Reconceptualizing and reorganizing the scholarly work of faculty members has only begun.

References

Benson, L., and Harkavy, I. "Community-Higher Education-School Partnerships as a Strategy to Realize the Democratic Promise of American Schooling and American Society." *Principal Leadership,* forthcoming.

Bok, D. *Universities and the Future of America.* Durham, N.C.: Duke University Press, 1990.

Boyer, E. L. "The New American Scholar." Keynote address presented at the AAHE National Conference on Higher Education, San Francisco, Apr. 1, 1990. (1990a)

Boyer, E. L. *Scholarship Reconsidered: Priorities of the Professoriate.* Menlo Park, Calif.: Carnegie Foundation for the Advancement of Teaching, 1990b.

Diamond, R., and Adam, B. (eds.). *The Disciplines Speak: Rewarding the Scholarly, Professional, and Creative Work of Faculty.* Washington, D.C.: American Association for Higher Education, 1995.

Diamond, R., and Adam, B. (eds.). *The Disciplines Speak II: More Statements on Rewarding the Scholarly, Professional, and Creative Work of Faculty.* Washington, D.C.: American Association for Higher Education, 2000.

Flexner, A. *Medical Education in the United States (The Flexner Report).* Menlo Park, Calif.: Carnegie Foundation for the Advancement of Teaching, 1910.

Gladwell, M. *The Tipping Point: How Little Things Can Make a Big Difference.* New York: Little, Brown, 2000.

Lynton, E. *Making a Case for Professional Service.* Washington, D.C.: American Association for Higher Education, 1995.

Lynton, E., and Driscoll, A. *Making Outreach Visible: A Guide to Documenting Professional Service and Outreach.* Washington, D.C.: American Association for Higher Education, 1999.

Rice, R. E., Sorcinelli, M. D., and Austin, A. E. *Heeding New Voices: Academic Careers for a New Generation.* Washington, D.C.: American Association for Higher Education, 2000.

Schon, D. A. *The Reflective Practitioner: How Professionals Think in Action.* New York: Basic Books, 1983.

Schon, D. A. "Knowing in Action. The New Scholarship Requires a New Epistemology." *Change,* 1995, 27(6), 27–34.

Seldin, P. *The Teaching Portfolio: A Practical Guide to Improved Performance and Promotion/Tenure Decisions* (2nd ed.). Bolton, MA: Anker Publishing Co., Inc., 1997.

Shulman, L. "Knowledge and Teaching: Foundations of the New Reform." *Harvard Educational Review,* 1987, 36(4), 1–22.

Sykes, C. J. *ProfScam: Professors and the Demise of Higher Education.* New York: St. Martin's Press, 1988.

Walshok, M. L. *Knowledge Without Boundaries: What America's Research Universities Can Do for the Economy, the Workplace, and the Community.* San Francisco: Jossey-Bass, 1995.

R. EUGENE RICE is scholar-in-residence at the American Association for Higher Education and director of AAHE's Forum on Faculty Roles and Rewards.

2

This chapter focuses on the influence of computers and communications technology on the scholarly process. Examples of this influence on all aspects of scholarship, from formulating ideas and gathering data to collaborating and publishing results, are discussed.

Transforming the Scholarly Process Through Information Technology

Wallace Hannum

Because of technology, the last few decades have witnessed a dramatic transformation in both the process and the power of scholarship. Today, capitalizing on the benefits of computers and communications technologies, scholars are accomplishing much more in less time, and are addressing problems heretofore unsolvable. Scholars in the sciences, for example, now use remarkably fast and powerful computers to analyze prodigious mountains of data, accomplishing in seconds what would have taken months when computations were done manually. Instead of laboriously scanning card catalogues for resources or being forced to spend considerable time and money in travel to distant libraries, where they would be spending even more time manually searching collections for needed documents, researchers now work through automated academic libraries that offer catalogues of their holdings, which are available on-line in a networked environment with other libraries. Indeed, scholars now have access to over forty million titles in the Online Computer Library Center (OCLC) catalogue, which is available worldwide. Just press the right keys and most of the classic works of literature, scholarly journals, and major newspapers will appear on the computer screen.

Consider a few other applications of technology to scholarship. Could we have the Human Genome Project without computers and communications technology? Could scholars explore human behavior as well without use of sophisticated computer simulations of social processes? Could art historians analyze completely a work of art without computer analysis of the digital images? Could archaeologists locate, excavate, and map ancient villages without computer technologies to guide them? Could historians find patterns and meaning in the vast, complex arrays of data available to

NEW DIRECTIONS FOR TEACHING AND LEARNING, no. 90, Summer 2002 © Wiley Periodicals, Inc.

them without computer analysis? Could scholars dialogue as actively as they presently do without discussion forums and e-mail? Technology, in short, has changed the very nature of scholarship by speeding the process and providing new tools that enable scholars to focus on new problems and challenges. But technology is not just enhancing scholarly productivity—by providing a way of doing more of the same work in less time; rather, it is leading to a paradigm shift in which scholars are able to work on or explore various problems in a fundamentally different fashion.

This chapter, then, examines how technology—that is, computer and other information technologies—has influenced the work of scholars, emphasizing its impact in particular on the scholarship of discovery and integration. Furthermore, this discussion is organized according to the common tasks of scholars: reviewing related research, seeking funding sources to support their work, collaborating with colleagues, collecting data, analyzing data, and communicating their findings.

Reviewing Related Research

In all disciplines, scholars initiate their work by becoming informed of the work of other scholars. Productive scholarship builds on and is informed by previously conducted related research. Of course, there is the occasional novel idea or new approach sometimes seen in scholarship, but, generally, work is evolutionary, extending previous research. Until recently, reviewing previous research meant spending days, weeks, or even months in a major academic library, poring over stacks of books and periodicals. Unless the scholar happened to be on the faculty of a major research university, a review of related research also meant travel to a library that had the requisite resources. Within the realm of the humanities, this meant travel to view the original work, not just travel to locate journal articles about the work. Access to resources restricted scholarship and limited the number of people who could engage in scholarly activities. Now, a vast array of scholarly work is available worldwide in digital form through the Internet. This has certainly made reviewing prior work more convenient, but it has also opened up access to many others to engage in scholarship.

The work of a scholar in reviewing related research has been made much easier and many times faster through information technology. On-line searches of electronic databases such as BIOSIS, EconLit, ERIC, Iter, LION, Medline, PsychLit, and Sociofile allow people anywhere to locate articles relevant to their own work in moments. Information technology has assisted scholars reviewing related research by helping them identify articles relevant to their work and obtain the full text copy of these articles. Many sources provide full text of articles on-line. Other sources provide faxed copies of articles within twenty-four hours. By allowing a faster and more comprehensive review of related literature, technology assists scholars in planning their own work.

Scholars are not limited to the use of general search engines such as Lycos, Altavista, or Google when looking for appropriate resources related to their scholarship on the Web. They may also use specialty sites with search engines and indices that are specific to their field and are peer-reviewed. For example, Argos is the first peer-reviewed search engine in a specialized area. Argos was designed to locate valuable resources related to ancient and medieval cultures. A team of international scholars ensures quality control through the peer review process. Literary Resources on the Net contains references to sites in English and American literature. REESWeb has information about resources on Central Asia and the former Soviet Union.

Information technology has also introduced more equity into scholarship by making necessary resources widely available to persons who do not happen to be at major research universities. This opens up the possibility of productive scholarship to people at smaller institutions without large periodical collections. It also opens up scholarship to people on continents other than North America and Europe, who may not have the resources of many large universities with good libraries. With many more people with more diverse backgrounds able to engage in reviewing related research, perhaps the quality of scholarship will be elevated as new ideas and new interpretations enter the stream.

Of course, things other than access to good libraries limit scholarship, so information technology alone will not guarantee immediate large-scale scholarly activities in areas in which scholarship was heretofore uncommon. Still, information technology will allow immediate access to the digital resources of the Internet to anyone with a connection anywhere in the world. This provides multiple opportunities for enhancing scholarship through improved reviews of previous research.

Locating Funding Sources

An age-old problem of scholars has been finding financial support for their work. This continues to the current day, even with numerous governmental, philanthropic, and corporate sources for funding. The marketplace for funding has never been overly efficient, making it difficult, if not impossible, for those people seeking funding to locate those who provide funding opportunities. In the past, word of mouth was often the primary way in which information about funding opportunities flowed. Under these conditions, a few scholars acquired information about funding sources, and the funding sources acquired information about a few scholars who were doing work related to their funding interests. Consequently, many opportunities were not realized because of the inefficient market.

In a number of ways, technology has introduced more efficiency into the marketplace for funding. Most funding sources, both public and private, maintain Web sites that provide viewers with information about their funding opportunities. Organizations provide information about their missions, their current funding goals, past projects they have supported, recent solicitations for funding, and points of contact. This has made it easy to locate potential funding sources that have stated interests in the area of a scholar's work. Several guides to funding sources are available on-line as well. One classic source is *A Grant Seeker's Guide to the Internet: Revised and Revisited* (http://www.mindspring.com/~ajgrant/guide.htm). The Federal Register, which publishes information from federal agencies daily, and the *Chronicle of Philanthropy*, which publishes weekly information from nonprofits, are also available on-line. Numerous sites have information to assist those who are developing proposals for funding. These sites include The Foundation Center's site (http://fdncenter.org) and the Grantsmanship Center site (http://www.tgci.com), both of which explain the grant development process, including locating potential funding sources.

Perhaps the best example of information technology applied to the task of locating potential funding sources is a service such as the "Community of Scholars," which scans funding opportunities in its database on a regular basis and automatically informs one of potential funding opportunities that match one's research interests. The Illinois Researcher Information Service (IRIS) (http://gateway.library.uicu.edu/iris) sends funding alerts via e-mail to users, as does "Fedixopportunity Alert" (http://content.science-wise.com/fedix), which sends e-mail announcements about grant opportunities from federal agencies. The American Association for the Advancement of Science sponsors "EurekAlert" (http://www.eurekalert.org), a site that has information about grants in the sciences. In order to participate in services like these, one must first establish a profile of one's research interests, and then funding opportunities are compared against this profile to identify those opportunities that may be appropriate. All of these operate to facilitate the flow of information about funding sources to scholars. In sum, just as technology has given access to information in research libraries to a much wider audience, so has it widened access to funding information. Scholars outside the loop of a specific funding source now have access to information about funding opportunities from that funding source.

Collaborating with Other Scholars

Although significant research has been accomplished by single scholars working alone, much of today's research is the result of collaborative efforts. Technology has created opportunities for collaboration that did not previously exist. E-mail allows scholars separated by distance and time to communicate almost effortlessly. Discussion forums and chat rooms allow groups of scholars to exchange information and participate in ongoing dialogues about their research. Location is no longer a prerequisite for collaboration, as technology provides ways for scholars working at separate locations, even on separate continents, to communicate and share documents (Williges, 1998).

Beginning with the more widespread use of e-mail in the 1980s, discussion lists and bulletin boards have allowed scholars to post information and read comments from others. One such forum is the Humanist, for scholars interested in applications of technology to the humanities. Rutgers University and King's College London jointly operate this discussion forum. Some discussion forums, such as PHIL-LIT, ARCH-L, and H-NET, are specific to an academic domain—in this case philosophy, archaeology, and history, respectively. Other discussion forums generate conversations among scholars in different academic fields. For example, AUSTEN-L contains discussions of English literature, history, and gender studies. PSYCHE-D opens discussion of human consciousness to scholars with backgrounds in cognitive science, neuroscience, philosophy, and other disciplines. Technology used in this manner, to bring people interested in a common topic together for discussion, fosters collaboration among scholars who might otherwise miss this opportunity.

Another form of collaboration made possible through technology is the shared development of papers. Groupware allows persons at different locations to work on the same document in a shared workspace (Udell, 2001). The shared space can contain text, images, voice, and video—all of which are accessible to those collaborating, regardless of physical location. One archeologist may sketch her image representing a building for which ruins are being excavated, and her colleague, working in another country, immediately sees this and adds his view of what the building probably looked like. Using groupware, different scholars can work with the same text and images, allowing all of them to see any modification. Internet Relay Chat (IRC) allows real-time interaction among people in a text-based environment. Multiuser spaces support interactions among several people. Scholars use these technologies to collaborate and discuss issues of mutual interest. With National Endowment for the Humanities support, the Vroma Project establishes a multiuser space where people can meet and access databases, texts, and images related to the study of Roman culture. This affords a rich means of collaboration.

The social nature of work is changing through the options offered by technology (Kling, 1996). At first glance, the openness offered by discussion forums and chats would seem to be a democratizing influence on scholarly activities, therefore allowing for wider participation. However, research on computer-mediated communications tempers such optimism (Herring, 1993). Unfortunately, some of the same domination of conversation we experience in face-to-face meetings occurs on-line as well. Technology allows for more widespread communication and collaboration, but it does not guarantee success.

Collecting Data

Scholars in a variety of fields routinely collect data as part of their research efforts. The data may be people's responses to a survey about water pollution or political candidates, measurements of forces operating on an aircraft, the movements of certain animals, observations on the interaction of mothers and babies, the chemical composition of some manufacturing byproducts, references to some event in novels by a particular author, the feeding habits of lemurs, or any number of other possibilities. In most cases, a scholar's collection of data in his or her research has been improved through the use of technology. Most research organizations routinely collect survey data by using several technologies, including computer-assisted face-to-face interviewing, computer-assisted telephone interviewing, computerized self-administered questionnaires, voice recognition software, and electronic diaries (de Leeuw and Nicholls, 1996). These survey or interview data are routinely collected and entered directly into databases for analysis and record keeping. Researchers use personal digital assistants to gather field notes, which eliminates the need to transcribe their notes later. In the sciences, scholars use probes and sensors of various types to collect data, which can then be transmitted over networks, including wireless networks. Objects or animals being studied can be fitted with sensors and transmitters to automatically send data back to the researchers' offices.

Edyburn (1999) describes several ways technology facilitates data collection, including the use of hand-held data input devices, portable keyboards, data collection probes, bar code scanning, utility software that runs in the background and monitors user input, Web-based surveys, voice recognition, and digital cameras. Researchers use digital cameras to observe and record research subjects, whether human or animal, in a variety of situations, allowing for the collection of data that would have been difficult to gather otherwise. When technology is used to assist in data collection, not only are more data gathered in an efficient manner, but data that previously would have been unavailable can be collected.

Analyzing Data

The most obvious use of technology in the scholarly process, and one of the earliest uses, is computer analysis of data—particularly quantitative data. In the past, scholars would labor with statistical formulas and manual calculating devices for weeks to complete a sophisticated statistical analysis of research findings. Today, a reasonably well-equipped PC running statistical software can complete very sophisticated statistical analyses of data in moments. Thus, the task of data analysis has been greatly simplified by modern computers and software packages. This in turn has reduced the time scholars spend analyzing data and it has allowed a consideration of problems that previously were too complex. New discoveries are attributable to this ability of technology to analyze complex data, whether quantitative or qualitative. Kenny's study of Aristotle's *Ethics,* made possible through computer analysis, led him to conclude that books long considered to belong to both Nicomachean Ethics and Eudemian Ethics actually belonged only to Eudemian Ethics (Pavliscak, Ross, and Henry, 1997).

Technology has allowed scholars in the humanities to establish authorship of primary materials and to trace relationships among works and ideas.

The Internet has provided new means for data analysis. Pezzullo (2001) lists almost four hundred Web pages that perform interactive statistical calculations of all types. Previously, a scholar had to be at a major university computing center to perform complex statistical analysis, but, today, scholars anywhere in the world with an Internet connection have access to substantial statistical analysis capability. Furthermore, through technology, scholars have access to guidance and assistance, including expert system software, to help them determine how to analyze their data. Technology has made available the computation power to perform data analysis and the expertise to determine the best approach to analyzing data in a given circumstance.

Communicating Research Results

A hallmark of scholarship continues to be the publication and communication of one's ideas and findings. The peer-reviewed article represents the essence of scholarly accomplishment in most fields. The value of peer-review publication remains, but the form is changing because of technology. An obvious change has been the rise of electronic publications, particularly e-journals, which are available over the Internet. The number of e-journals now numbers over seventeen hundred. Print journals remain, but the high cost of publication, along with limited markets for specialized scholarly journals, has placed the emphasis on e-journals. Some have argued that the e-journal will replace print journals (Hibbitts, 1996). Even if traditional print journals prevail, technology has had an impact on them as well. Scholars collaborate on publications by sending drafts back and forth as attachments to e-mail. Articles are submitted electronically to editors and reviewers with comments returned electronically. This shortens the time for writing and publication.

Electronic publication of scholarly articles and reports has been a natural use of the Internet, and it was, after all, developed in academic and related research and development communities in which scholarly dissemination and publication of knowledge is prized (Kling, 1996). But people hold mixed opinions about the value of e-journals. Okerson (1991) argues that e-journals should become valuable forms of scholarly communication. In some fields, this seems to have happened. For example, Kling (1996) has noted that in high-energy physics, electronic publishing is well organized and accepted. Physicists, like other scientists, build on work in other labs as they attempt to establish themselves with new discoveries or inventions. In a competitive research environment, being first to introduce new findings promises greater rewards and recognition. With a publication lag in academic journals of up to two years from the date of submission, scientists working on the frontier of research must be reading early versions—that is, preprints—of others' work on the Web, and they are presenting early versions of their work on their Web sites and in e-journals to establish their work. This confirms Okerson's observations about the growing importance of e-journals.

Arguing from a different point of view, Gregorian (1994) cautions that the quantity and speed of scholarly communication made available by technology comes with a price. That price, Gregorian claims, is fragmentation of knowledge and increased specialization in academic disciplines, which will lead us away from a community like the global village McLuhan predicted, toward something more like the worst of urban life, in which we retreat into smaller communities of like-minded people who avoid dealing with others who are not exactly like them. This view stands in contrast with that expressed by Bennett (1996), who argued that technology will have the opposite effect on scholars by connecting them more broadly with scholars in other disciplines and with scholars internationally.

Conclusion

Perhaps we are in a time in which the distinction between scholars who have integrated technology fully into their work and those who have not has become more important than the distinction within the academy between the sciences and the humanities. As Kenny (1999) indicates, we may be developing a new cultural gap that will rival the two cultures C. P. Snow identified. This new cultural gap is between computer-using academics and non-computer-using academics.

Computer and information technology has the potential for dramatic impact on scholars and scholarship. Lougee (2001) has discussed the impact technology may have on academic life, in terms of both research and teaching. She argues that technology is forcing us to reevaluate such concerns of scholarship as, how we count publication in e-journals, how we participate in scholarly debate via electronic networks, and how we create our databases. More broadly, she suggests that technology may profoundly change the university.

The impact of computer and information technologies on scholarship has begun and is growing. Certainly, scholars can do more work and do it more quickly with technology. Considerable evidence exists that suggests that technology enables scholars to consider and grapple with problems and issues different from those they were previously able to consider and work on. Technology has already altered how scholars work and the problems on which they work. Whom scholars work with and whom they work for may well change through technology. Computer and communications technologies have affected all aspects of the research process. Most observers note this as a positive occurrence, an enhancement of scholarship, whereas others point to possible undesirable effects and question our embracing of technology. However, even the opponents of widespread technology application in universities are not asking to turn the clock back and eliminate technology. They are pointing to some limitations and some negative influences that may arise. With proper attention to these concerns, computer and communications technologies should have a growing impact on scholarship as we move forward.

References

Bennett, D. C. "New Connections for Scholars: The Changing Missions of a Learned Society in an Era of Digital Networks." Occasional Paper Series, no. 36. American Council of Learned Societies, 1996.

de Leeuw, E., and Nicholls, W. "Technological Innovations in Data Collection: Acceptance, Data Quality and Costs." *Sociological Research Online,* 1996, 1(4).

Edyburn, D. L. *The Electronic Scholar.* Englewood Cliffs, N.J.: Prentice Hall, 1999.

Gregorian, V. "Technology, Scholarship and the Humanities: Implications of the Electronic Age." *Leonardo,* 1994, 27(2), 155–164.

Herring, S. C. "Gender and Democracy in Computer Mediated Communications." *Electronic Journal of Communication,* 1993, 3(2).

Hibbitts, B. J. "Last Writes: Reassessing the Law Review on the Age of Cyberspace." *New York University Law Review,* 1996, 71(3), 615–688.

Kenny, A. "Scholarship and Information Technology." In Terry Coppock (ed.), *Information Technology and Scholarship.* Oxford: Oxford University Press, 1999.

Kling, B. *Computerization and Controversy: Value Conflicts and Social Choices* (2nd ed.). Orlando, Fla.: Academic Press, 1996.

Lougee, C. C. "Technology, Scholarship and the Humanities: The Implications of Electronic Information." [http://www.cni.org/docs/tsh/Lougee.html]. July 2001.

Okerson, A. "The Electronic Journal: What, Whence, And When?" *The Public-Access Computer Systems Review,* 1991, 1(2), 5–24.

Pavliscak, P., Ross, S., and Henry, C. "Information Technology in Humanities Scholarship: Achievements, Prospects, and Challenges—The United States Focus." Occasional Paper Series, no. 37. American Council of Learned Societies, 1997.

Pezzullo, J. "Interactive Statistical Pages." [http://members.aol.com/johnp71/javastat.html]. July 2001.

Udell, J. "Internet Groupware for Scientific Collaboration." [http://software-carpentry.codesourcery.com/Groupware/report.html]. July 2001.

Williges, R.C. "Advancing Scholarly Research Through the Electronic World." Blacksburg, Va.: Virginia Polytechnic Institute and State University, Hypermedia Technical Report HCIL-96–01, 1998.

WALLACE HANNUM is an associate professor of education at the University of North Carolina at Chapel Hill.

3

Institution-wide cultures of hope and opportunity help encourage, nurture, and support scholarship. This chapter identifies the prerequisites for creating such an environment, discusses the intrainstitutional partnerships that promote scholarship, and lists some of the benefits accruing from the resulting gestalt.

Nurturing Scholarship Through Holistic Faculty Development: A Synergistic Approach

Kenneth J. Zahorski

In C. S. Lewis's classic science fiction novel, *Out of the Silent Planet,* the protagonist, Elwin Ransom, while on a walking tour in a remote part of England, is kidnapped, drugged, and then dragged aboard a spaceship headed for Malacandra (Mars). While en route, Ransom makes an astounding discovery: space is not merely a dark, dead void but rather "an Empyrean ocean of radiance" (Lewis, 1965, p. 32), a place of heavenly beauty alive with almost palpable brightness. Thus, rather than being overcome with dread and fear, he experiences an indescribable joy, a "sweet influence pouring . . . into his surrendered body" (p. 31). Perhaps most surprising is the source of Ransom's joy—space and what permeates it. In this chapter I also consider the power of space, or, more precisely, the power of space when infused with a nurturing spirit. However, it is not outer space I intend to explore but rather that familiar space in which we live our professional lives—the college or university campus. I contend that institutional space, a campus's cultural ether, can also be filled with a "sweet influence" capable of encouraging, nurturing, supporting, and sustaining scholarship among faculty members in all stages of their careers.

But just how do we go about creating an institution-wide culture of hope and opportunity capable of promoting and supporting scholarship? In this chapter I suggest a possible approach based on the experience I have had over the past seventeen years as director of a holistic faculty development program. It is an approach based on the premise that whereas individual components of a faculty development program do help foster and support scholarship, even more powerful is the synergy resulting from components

NEW DIRECTIONS FOR TEACHING AND LEARNING, no. 90, Summer 2002 © Wiley Periodicals, Inc.

29

working together and interacting with other institutional agencies. In short, it is the resulting gestalt, the almost magical effect of the whole becoming greater than the sum of its parts, that really makes the difference, creating a transformative energy that permeates a campus culture.

In this chapter I describe a strategy for creating such a gestalt, first identifying the prerequisites for creating a nurturing environment for scholarship, then discussing some of the intrainstitutional partnerships that promote scholarly endeavors, and then, finally, listing some of the benefits derived from this holistic strategy. Most of my illustrative examples are drawn from my experience with the program I direct at St. Norbert College, a small, private liberal arts college of about 2,000 students and approximately 160 full-time tenure-track and adjunct instructors. But although the examples may have been generated by a program in an institution of a particular size and type, the strategies, approaches, and activities described are readily replicable in other types and sizes of institutions as well. Perhaps even more important, the overarching philosophy and undergirding tenets of the holistic approach also widely appertain.

Prerequisites for Creating a Nurturing Environment

Although creating a campus culture that nurtures and supports scholarship is not easy, if approached with energy, determination, and sensitivity, it can be done. Following are some of the prerequisites for creating such a nurturing environment.

Holistic Faculty Development Program. The faculty development program having the best chance of creating a transformative gestalt is one that casts its net wide, incorporating opportunities not only for instructional but also for organizational and personal development. The following components constituting the St. Norbert College Faculty Development Program are fairly typical of most holistic programs: (1) a resource center, (2) a new faculty orientation and mentor program, (3) a minigrant program, (4) sabbatical and released time programs, (5) an annual faculty development conference, (6) topical sessions and workshops, (7) a brown bag lunch discussion series, (8) a faculty exchange program, (9) a newsletter, (10) a book discussion series, (11) regional faculty development network membership, (12) travel funding, (13) a phased retirement program, (14) outstanding teaching, scholarship, and community service awards, (15) a visiting scholars program, and (16) individual counseling. In addition, holistic programs usually have a director/coordinator with released time and a faculty development committee that monitors faculty needs and administers faculty development activities. If such a holistic program is not in place in your institution, however, do not despair; a strong set of faculty development practices will also suffice, although attaining desired outcomes will probably be proportionate to the program's scope.

Faculty Development Across the Institution. Although the Office of Faculty Development naturally assumes primary responsibility for an institution's professional growth initiatives and programs, including those promoting scholarship, generating a nurturing climate institution-wide demands commitment, resolve, and participation from the entire academic community. Department and division chairs, associate deans, and even academic vice presidents should also serve as professional growth agents, with the understanding, of course, that the evaluative dimensions of their positions prescribe somewhat their roles as developmental agents. Even the institution's mission statement should be redrafted, if necessary, to formalize a collegewide commitment to supporting and nurturing the scholarly lives of faculty members.

Faculty Developer as Anthropologist and Change Agent. Faculty development agents intent on mining all possibilities for creating a nurturing institutional climate must concurrently assume two other roles: anthropologist and change agent. After all, how can one hope to offer constructive suggestions for change without getting to know the institution intimately, much as a skilled anthropologist gets to know a culture through careful observation and study? This demands a reading regimen that includes the college catalogue, faculty handbook and constitution, and materials coming out of important institutional units such as the library, the institutional development office, computer and media services, and admissions. In addition, one must closely study the institutional governance structure and committee system. Furthermore, it means periodically visiting other buildings and getting to know administrative and staff colleagues who are likely to be key players in the quest for creating a nurturing culture. The knowledge and understanding gained from this ethnographic approach translates into the ability to become a positive force in generating constructive change. In short, a faculty development practitioner hoping to have impact as a change agent must learn to move through the sometimes labyrinthine organizational structure with agility and confidence (Zahorski, 1993).

Bridge Building. Faculty development personnel must also become master bridge builders, continually forging strong working partnerships between the office of faculty development and other sectors of the college/university community. The knowledge gained through anthropological sleuthing is vital to this artful enterprise. Essential, too, is a strong set of interpersonal skills. Establishing liaisons with colleagues throughout the college community not only represents a key stage in the synergistic process but also helps create the spirit of community so vital to a healthy campus climate.

Support from Start to Finish. An institutional culture has little chance of becoming fully supportive of the scholarly enterprise if its support systems are fragmentary. Faculty development must provide nurturance, guidance, and support from the very beginning to the very end of the process. This linchpin concept demands more extensive commentary.

Let us look more closely, for example, at the sabbatical—perhaps the most brilliant celestial body in the professional development firmament. At first glance the sabbatical might seem confined to the leave period itself, but in reality important stages occur both before and after it. A nurturing culture will provide what is needed to carry out successfully not only the sabbatical project but also what is requisite for planning the project, sharing the results, and celebrating the project's completion. Like the mythical Midgard serpent, mouth firmly clamped on tail and encompassing the earth in an unbroken circle, the faculty development process must also form a complete cycle, helping colleagues from start to finish of the scholarly process, with a circuit so complete that the ending stage often emerges as a new beginning.

But let's look at the sabbatical process even more closely. When a faculty member begins thinking about the possibility of applying for a sabbatical leave, a visit to the office of a faculty development professional should be one of the first steps in the preapplication and planning process. Faculty development agents with some counseling experience can serve as dependable guides, helping their colleagues clarify goals and objectives, define the sabbatical project, and determine its feasibility. Furthermore, faculty development personnel can help find answers to questions about the institution's sabbatical policies and guidelines, the formal application process, and possible sources of in-house and external funding (Zahorski, 1994). The reflective and planning process should not be a solitary exercise, and a faculty development agent can ensure that it is not by being a good listener, counselor, and sounding board—and by being all these things in a confidential setting.

Even the application process can be facilitated through the helpful ministrations of faculty development agents. Most colleges/universities have well-defined sabbatical leave proposal formats; therefore, following the prescribed format closely, under the watchful eye of a discerning and knowledgeable colleague, can often make the difference between an application's approval and its rejection. At St. Norbert College, the director of faculty development provides applicants with a sabbatical handbook, as well as access to files of successful sabbatical proposals.

During the presabbatical preparation stage, the faculty development agent can help successful applicants in various ways, including finding and setting up a congenial work environment, arranging for research and study-abroad experiences, assisting in the gathering of background reading materials, and recommending a sabbatical adviser/mentor. Even the actual leave period can be made more productive and enriching through the careful pre-planning undertaken in collaboration with faculty development personnel. A well-informed guide might suggest such things as constructing a reasonably and comfortably paced timetable, remaining flexible, breaking away from regular professional routines and duties, and keeping a sabbatical diary or journal.

But the assistance should not end here—although, unfortunately, it often does. Many faculty members suffer varying degrees of reentry shock (Jarecky and Sandifer, 1986). Once again, a colleague cum faculty development agent can help ease reentry through counseling, including arranging for a "reentry-friendly" return semester—building a psychological adjustment period into the final few weeks of the sabbatical, devising strategies for prolonging the positive effects of the sabbatical, and helping make contingency and follow-through plans.

In addition, a faculty development agent can set up venues for sharing sabbatical findings. Postsabbatical reporting opportunities help keep the flames of enthusiasm that were kindled during the leave period burning brightly after the sabbatical leave has ended. A faculty development newsletter can also serve as a fine vehicle for disseminating a written sabbatical report or article, just as a brown bag session can serve as a fine venue for an oral report. Indeed, a newsletter might feature a series devoted to sabbatical accounts. Still another possibility is to publish a collection of sabbatical reports.

Practicing the Art of Encouragement. It is critically important that all professional growth practitioners, from directors of faculty development through department chairs to deans, be encouragers and nurturers. As Martha Sinetar stresses in *The Mentoring Spirit* (1998), as counselors and mentors and facilitators, we must all become "artists of encouragement" (p. 25). It is difficult to overemphasize the importance and impact of the personal note of commendation (no matter how brief), the smile of approval and expression of congratulations, or the words of solace and subsequent encouragement during the down times in one's professional career. Collectively, these small gestures profoundly enhance culture—reenergizing both the individual and the institution.

Intrainstitutional Liaisons and Partnerships

Intrainstitutional liaisons and partnerships both nurture and are nurtured by an environment of opportunity and support. Working together, the components of a holistic faculty development program can create synergy, as can the faculty development components working in partnership with other institutional offices and agencies. The following examples are meant to be illustrative, not exhaustive. The potential for synergistic partnerships is limited only by the level of imagination, innovativeness, and industriousness of the faculty development professional.

Research Support. An office of faculty development can be of tremendous help to scholars by making the resource center a well-equipped scholar-writer's way station, making available key reference works on writing, editing, and publishing—including style manuals, guides for writing with word processors and preparing electronic manuscripts, and handbooks on such topics as nonsexist writing, copyright laws, research theory and practice, business reports, scientific papers, newsletters, editing, proposal writing, desktop publishing, and text design. Valuable enough in itself, such a collection takes on even greater value and accessibility when, in cooperation with the campus library, the resource center holdings are cross-listed in the central library's on-line catalogue. At St. Norbert College, the nearly two thousand items housed in the resource center are made available through WebPac, the Todd Wehr Library's on-line catalogue, with the result of far greater use of center materials. But this is not the only kind of partnership the faculty development office can forge with the library. Given the exponential changes occurring within the realm of information-gathering technology, scholars sometimes need guidance in how to take full advantage of their library's electronic resources. Periodic faculty development-sponsored information sessions, featuring reference librarians describing the latest research technology, can be invaluable to scholars seeking efficient and relatively inexpensive research procedures.

Grant Writing Guidance and Support. Just as a faculty development resource center can help scholars with research and writing, so, too, can it serve as a solid launching pad for grant writing and research. St. Norbert College faculty members needing information on external sources of financial support can regularly consult the resource center's Grant Registry File, which holds information in alphabetically arranged folders on over 100 foundations and granting agencies. Complementing the registry are several excellent reference and "how-to" texts. In addition, the center houses up-to-date information on all internal funding sources, including official guidelines and application forms, as well as complete sets of successful grant applications.

The search for grant funding and the writing of grants is a complex and challenging endeavor; applicants need all the help they can get. Faculty development personnel can help, as can the materials housed in an office of faculty development. But this help can be made far more potent when it is bolstered by the resources of an office of institutional development. Offices of faculty and institutional development working together in close partnership can provide scholars with much more help than can each unit working independently. What a faculty development resource center does not have in the way of materials, the institutional advancement office probably will have, and both offices can stretch always scarce human resources by joining forces. In addition, the institutional development office often possesses more tools and expertise for conducting comprehensive searches for external funding sources—including government, foundation, and corporate agencies—than the usually smaller faculty development office. The faculty development office can start the process and perhaps even supply the start-up funds needed for a research project; the institutional development office can then advance the process in both areas.

However, the partnering need not stop here. Faculty development should also work closely with other institutional units, such as the international education office. Here is one example of how this might work. A few years ago, during the fall semester, the St. Norbert College Office of Faculty Development devoted its entire "Food for Thought" brown bag luncheon series to the topic "Growing Through Grants," taking advantage of the knowledge of those scholars who had recently received support through grants from international funding agencies. During the following semester, the Office of Faculty Development and the International Center cospon-sored a workshop on the Fulbright Scholar Program. The presentation team consisted of the associate director of the International Center and a profes-sor of history who had recently returned from a Fulbright semester. The workshop, well attended and reportedly helpful, emblematized synergistic partnering.

Collaborative Scholarship Opportunities. Most scholarship benefits from collaboration, but partnerships are seldom formed by chance. Initiatives, programs, and encouragement are often needed to promote and nurture the team approach. Sometimes the synergy results from complementarity, with one program supporting and nourishing another merely by coexisting with it. At St. Norbert College a great deal of collaboration goes on not only between peers but also between faculty members and students, in large part because there are so many coexisting units that encourage and support such partnerships. The Office of Faculty Development, for example, provides in-house funding for a broad spectrum of collaborative projects, from three funding sources, concurrent with divisional and departmental initiatives.

One of the funds administered by the Office of Faculty Development is especially designed to promote student-faculty scholarly, pedagogical, artis-tic, and curricular collaborations. Initiated by the graduating class of 1986, the Student-Faculty Development Endowment Fund now offers eleven thousand-dollar awards yearly. Periodically, the Division of Humanities and Fine Arts also offers funding for student-faculty scholarly projects, and the Office of Admissions recently inaugurated the Research Fellows Program, offering several first-year students opportunities to conduct research with faculty mentors. By pairing each participating incoming student with a fac-ulty mentor, this pilot program not only helps students develop meaning-ful relationships with faculty members, it also supports faculty research efforts already in progress that need additional support. All these initiatives, emanating from different units but working together harmoniously, have resulted in a gestalt that has made student-faculty research partnerships an institutional hallmark.

Monetary and Released Time Support. As travel and conference expenses continue to increase, faculty members often have difficulty find-ing sufficient funds to maintain their scholarly agendas. Although mini-grants relieve some of the strain on personal budgets, many faculty members simply cannot afford to make conference trips to distant U.S. cities, let alone international destinations, even if the trip represents an excellent opportunity to further their professional career. One way of ame-liorating the situation is to combine departmental and divisional travel funds with faculty development in-house grants. This blending of resources often makes it possible for faculty members to deliver papers and conduct other scholarly business off-campus. In short, the possibility of combining monetary and other such resources generates many opportunities that wouldn't have existed if only one source of support were available.

Sharing and Celebrating Scholarship. One of the long-standing components of St. Norbert College's faculty development program is an event called "Celebrating Collegiality." The foundational concept is simple: because faculty members are separated by disciplines and buildings, agenda-free social activities drawing colleagues together for interaction that helps nurture collegiality and community are warmly welcomed. The event, set in a comfortable room, late in the afternoon, features live piano music and plenty of good food and drink. Mellowed by candlelight and soft background music, faculty members chat and forget, for at least two hours or so, the papers, committee assignments, and lecture notes back on their office desks. This well-attended and highly successful event becomes even more meaningful when combined with a closely related activity event, sponsored by the dean of the college, called "Celebrating Scholarship." In an adjoining room, on tables lining the walls, displays of faculty scholarship, ranging from articles and books to computer software packages and videotape productions, are displayed. Faculty members leisurely move from one room to another, sipping refreshments and carrying on conversations while examining the scholarly achievements of their colleagues. This is but another example of how separate units can work together toward creating something more enriching and powerful than could be achieved in isolation. The Office of Faculty Development can also sponsor joint projects with particular departments and divisions, or it can even go beyond the campus to work collaboratively with sister institutions through regional networks. The possibilities are boundless.

Benefits Derived

Many benefits derive from creating a nurturing and supportive climate for scholarship. Most obvious, of course, is a higher level of scholarly productivity. But there are other benefits as well, many of them not as tangible as increased productivity but in their own way fully as significant. First of all, in the synergistic model previously described, an office of faculty development becomes a more potent institutional force because of the additional clout and visibility gained from the alliances forged with other institutional units. In brief, faculty development components powerful in themselves become even more potent transforming agents when collaborating harmoniously with other institutional programs and offices. Second, through the intrainstitutional liaisons and partnerships characteristic of the synergistic approach, stronger bridges are built between faculty development and other institutional entities. Enhanced collaboration means enhanced communication, ultimately resulting in a revitalized spirit of collegiality and community. Third, through a synergistic approach, the importance of other professional growth agents and agencies outside the office of faculty development is accentuated. The awareness that professional growth is everyone's business can lead to much positive change on any campus. Indeed, faculty development is always most effective when it becomes an organic part of an institution and when it becomes part of the institutional fabric. Finally, and perhaps most important, the synergistic approach helps create an environment of hope and opportunity, the kind of environment in which scholarship has the best chance of thriving.

Conclusion

If the components of a holistic faculty development program perform their functions well, while concurrently forming a synergistic dynamic with other institutional agents, a college's or university's cultural environment need not be a lifeless vacuity but, rather, like the dynamic space Elwin Ransom discovers while journeying to Malacandra, it can be a living, nurturing environment that lifts the spirits, engenders hope, encourages and supports risk taking and innovation, and inculcates a spirit of cooperation and collaboration. Just as Ransom is made better by the "sweet influence" of the space through which he passes, so, too, is the scholar encouraged, nurtured, and supported through the sweet influence of a beneficent campus environment. And, like Ransom, faculty development professionals must try to gain a new vision of space. Ransom experiences a reeducation, a fresh perspective, as he speeds toward Mars and a series of epiphanic, life-changing experiences, once he arrives on the red planet. Although our professional journeys may not be nearly as dramatic as Ransom's, we do have the opportunity to effect dramatic change on our campuses if we are willing to become catalytic change agents in the quest to create healthier environments in which scholars and scholarship may grow and prosper. The promise of better things lies in the very space surrounding us, but in order to fulfill that promise, we must first recognize it.

References

Jarecky, R., and Sandifer, M. "Faculty Members' Evaluations of Sabbaticals." *Journal of Medical Education,* 1986, *61*(10), 803–807.

Lewis, C.S. *Out of the Silent Planet.* New York: The Macmillan Co., 1965.

Sinetar, M. *The Mentoring Spirit: Life Lessons on Leadership and the Art of Encouragement.* New York: St. Martin's Press, 1998.

Zahorski, K. J. "Taking the Lead: Faculty Development as Institutional Change Agent." In D. L. Wright and J. P. Lunde (eds.), *To Improve the Academy.* Vol. 12. Stillwater, Okla.: New Forums Press, 1993.

Zahorski, K. J. *The Sabbatical Mentor: A Practical Guide to Successful Sabbaticals.* Bolton, Mass.: Anker, 1994.

KENNETH J. ZAHORSKI is professor of English and director of faculty development at St. Norbert College, De Pere, Wisconsin.

PART TWO

New Values

4

Scholarship Reconsidered *gave us an amplified vision of scholarly work, yet the process of tenure has inhibited the full realization of that vision. This chapter argues that we need to make the tenure process work more effectively and flexibly in order to validate and encourage the multiple types of scholarship Boyer proposes.*

New Conceptions of Scholarship for a New Generation of Faculty Members

Mary Deane Sorcinelli

Over the past decade, four-year institutions, particularly research universities and the larger comprehensive institutions with complex missions, have been subject to criticism centering on issues of faculty work. Simply put, constituencies inside and outside universities have argued that faculty members are spending too much time on disciplinary-based research and are ignoring both undergraduate students and the broader society. In 1990, when Ernest Boyer produced his seminal work, *Scholarship Reconsidered,* it was hailed as a breakthrough in the understanding of faculty work. The goal of *Scholarship Reconsidered* was to move beyond the debate over "teaching versus research" as faculty priorities in order to give scholarly work a more efficacious and enlarged meaning. Boyer proposed four forms of scholarship that should be valued equally: discovery, integration, engagement, and teaching and learning.

On campuses across the nation, faculty members and administrators have discussed this new paradigm of scholarship with great seriousness. For example, on my own campus I served on a multiyear, campuswide Task Force on Faculty Roles and Rewards, which looked at these different formulations of scholarship and provided recommendations with regard to personnel policies. In addition, national interest has sustained ten years of annual conferences on "Faculty Roles and Rewards," sponsored by the American Association of Higher Education, as well as a range of reform efforts, such as the scholarship of teaching, the peer review of teaching, the assessment of student learning, and standards for assessing scholarship (Glassick, Huber and Maeroff, 1997; Hutchings, 1996; Hutchings and Shulman, 1999).

NEW DIRECTIONS FOR TEACHING AND LEARNING, no. 90, Summer 2002 © Wiley Periodicals, Inc.

During the same decade, researchers conducted several notable studies of doctoral candidates considering academic careers, graduates on the job market, and new and early-career faculty members in tenure-track appointments (Boice, 1992; Menges, 1999; Rice, Sorcinelli, and Austin, 2000; Sorcinelli and Austin, 1992; Tierney and Bensimon, 1996; Trower, 2001). Taken together, these studies suggest that personnel policies and other rewards and incentive systems continue to place a heavy emphasis on research. Although *Scholarship Reconsidered* (Boyer, 1990) has broadened the debate about "research versus teaching" and has truly influenced the lives of teachers on a number of campuses, discussions with early-career faculty members have revealed that Boyer's vision of greater parity among the scholarships has yet to be fully realized. *Scholarship Reconsidered*'s goal of integrating personal and institutional endeavors and providing a wholeness to scholarly work has bumped up against a tenure system that early-career faculty members characterize as "our greatest barrier to a better future" (Rice, 1996).

In this chapter I briefly describe criticisms of the current tenure process and the ways in which the process impedes realization of Boyer's vision. I then explore some encouraging changes that directly address flaws in the tenure process and work to more effectively and flexibly validate and encourage the multiple types of scholarship that Boyer has proposed.

Tension Between Ideals and Reality

Although there have been a number of studies of aspiring and new faculty members, these studies commonly ask one broad question: How do doctoral students and early-career faculty members experience their graduate education, the job search process, and the tenure track? And, in answering, young scholars commonly describe a tension they experience between ideals and reality as they move through graduate school and into faculty posts. They struggle to balance their ideals about life in the academy with tenure and the realities of doing meaningful work and trying to lead a balanced life. Once hired, many early-career faculty members reported experiencing an incomprehensible tenure system, a lack of community, and an unbalanced life. One study (Rice, Sorcinelli, and Austin, 2000), which was grounded in structured interviews with more than 350 aspiring and early-career faculty members, focused directly on perceptions of the tenure process.

Key Concerns with the Tenure Process

Although many early-career faculty members expressed reservations about the tenure system as a whole, most identified the *process* of contending for tenure as their most urgent concern (Rice, Sorcinelli, and Austin, 2000). *Expectations for performance* on the tenure track were described as ambiguous, shifting, and inconsistent. Even more worrisome to interviewees were ever-escalating expectations. Across nearly all disciplines and sectors of higher education, early-career faculty members described a "raising of the bar" and a "ratcheting up" of requirements for tenure, especially in research. Many received *little formal feedback or mentoring* from senior colleagues. They were disappointed not to find a long-anticipated, supportive community of senior scholars, a department chair, and students. And tenure-track faculty members themselves were reluctant to seek assistance because doing so was tantamount to admitting a weakness.

To compound the problem, the *collegial review structure* is flawed. The lineup of decision makers includes frequently rotating chairs and a personnel committee with rapid turnover of its members. And although tenure requirements and processes may in some cases be spelled out in policy language, most of those interviewed had no clear understanding of how the actual process worked, exactly who was involved, or how to compile their dossiers.

Finally, the *tenure time line* has a short-term focus, whereas scholars' passions require a long-term view. The tenure process was described as inflexible and unresponsive to decreased funding, publication backlogs, the learning curve for teaching and preparing courses, the time needed to exploit the advantages of new technologies, and the personal demands made on scholars struggling to balance their lives.

In sum, the young scholars we interviewed were asking for changes in the tenure process that reflect much of what *Scholarship Reconsidered* imagined: the conceptualization of teaching and community engagement as scholarly enterprises; rich, public, collegial discourse about teaching, student learning, and civic commitments on- and off-campus; and opportunities to work flexibly and collaboratively, finding intellectual and supportive colleagueship across the disciplines.

Improving the Tenure Process

Scholarship Reconsidered opened up the conversation about faculty reward structures in disciplines and at campuses across the country. Indeed, Boyer has directly addressed the tenure process and has urged the academy to encourage and reward all four categories of scholarly work. And although the academy remains firmly committed to research and discovery, it has taken steps to reaffirm its historic mission of teaching and seeking new ways to promote public engagement. Briefly described are some exemplars from campuses that have been developing practices and policies that respond to some of the most fundamental concerns about the tenure process (Sorcinelli, 2000).

Communicating Expectations for Performance. Early-career faculty members need to know what is expected of them, and departments, schools, and colleges have adopted various practices to make this information accessible. Arizona State University's College of Liberal Arts and Sciences has instituted a model of faculty work in which responsibilities are negotiable and flexible, and the College encourages the integration of different forms of scholarly work. The College is now developing a formal system for evaluating both individual and unit accomplishments. Portland State University engages its faculty in both the scholarship of teaching and the scholarship of community-based learning and provides models for documenting these new forms of scholarship in promotion and tenure portfolios.

Giving Feedback on Progress. Early-career faculty members seek clear and constructive performance feedback. The Promotion and Tenure Committee at Indiana University–South Bend offers voluntary third-year reviews by peers to all tenure-track faculty members to provide confidential, formative feedback at a time when it can be most helpful. One college dean at the University of Wisconsin–Steven's Point brings pretenure faculty members together annually to solicit suggestions for improving life on the tenure track. Centers for teaching and learning often offer services that help newcomers assess their own teaching and their students' learning. Our Center for Teaching, for example, offers all first-year faculty members the opportunity to collect feedback from their students at midterm and to begin preparing a philosophy of teaching statement and teaching portfolio (Mues and Sorcinelli, 2000). These initiatives all serve to encourage conversation about career development, to promote informed and supportive peer review, and to advance an amplified vision of scholarship, especially the scholarship of teaching.

Enhancing Collegial Review Processes. Early-career faculty members desire more ongoing discussion in the department or college of the tenure process and the values that inform it. A college dean at Drake University annually brings together the probationary faculty members and the college tenure review committee, and committee members share information on their composition, charge, and review process. At the University of Washington, the oceanography department invites junior faculty members to observe tenure reviews in order to demystify the process ("The Future of Tenure: Interview with Richard Chait," 1999). In a special program for minority faculty members, Eastern Michigan University conducts an orientation in which tenured faculty members of color offer advice to and answer questions from the recently appointed tenure-track minority faculty members. These kinds of collegial discussions make public the process of tenure and allow early-career faculty members and their departments to better assess the progress of their scholarly work, in whatever form it takes.

Creating Flexible Timelines for Tenure. Some campuses are beginning to allow some flexibility in the timing of the tenure review. At Marquette University, an early-career faculty member who becomes a parent during the probationary period can "stop the clock" for one year. Conversely, chairs at a range of institutions—such as Northwestern University, College of Charleston, and Saint Olaf College—can "move the clock forward" by working within the institutional framework to award newcomers credit for prior college teaching experience. These initiatives confirm that scholarly work takes considerable time and effort if it is to embody the dimensions that Glassick, Huber, and Maeroff (1997) posited: clear goals, adequate preparation, appropriate methods, significant results, effective presentation, and reflective critique.

Encouraging Mentoring by Senior Faculty Members. On many campuses, the interaction between senior faculty members and newcomers has been too limited, particularly around the tenure process. Mindful of this gulf, Colorado College assigns each new tenure-track faculty member to a senior or retired faculty member outside the newcomer's department, and the two meet monthly to discuss career development issues. At Kean University, new faculty members receive a one-course reduction during the first semester so that they can participate in a mentoring program featuring distinguished senior colleagues appointed as "Presidential Teaching Scholars." At Brigham Young University, the orientation of new faculty members is a year-long program involving a structured mentoring relationship with a senior faculty member and an intensive two-week learning experience in which new faculty members work individually, with one another, and with experienced faculty members and administrators. These exemplars of mentoring and support encourage the setting of goals among the four scholarships and a plan for achieving them that can be shared in collegial dialogue with mentors.

Preparing the Future Professoriate. We need to duplicate for graduate students many of the supportive activities offered to new faculty members. Fortunately, there is a major national initiative involving many of the research universities where aspiring faculty members are prepared. The Preparing Future Faculty project, sponsored by the Association of American Colleges and Universities and the Council of Graduate Schools, cultivates a broader conception of scholarly work. The project has developed a number of model programs to better prepare graduate students interested in academic careers (Tice, Gaff, and Pruitt-Logan, 1998).

For example, Howard University awards a Certificate in College and University Faculty Preparation to those who satisfactorily complete a two-year, faculty-supervised preparatory program consisting of a course called Preparing for the Professoriate, a week-long training in distance learning techniques, and periodic symposia on issues affecting higher education. At the University of Minnesota, the program places graduate students aspiring to faculty careers directly into the different settings in which the profession is practiced. Graduate students are introduced to institutions with different missions, student profiles, and faculty responsibilities. Such "preparing the future professoriate" initiatives allow aspiring teachers to assess the full range of scholarly work in which faculty members engage at community colleges, liberal arts colleges, and comprehensive and research universities.

Recognizing the Department Chair as Career Sponsor. Interviews with early-career faculty members returned repeatedly to the pivotal role department chairs play in the tenure and promotion process. Flawed tenure processes can exact a heavy toll on the candidate, department, and institution. There are a number of recent initiatives that provide chairs with guidance on supporting early-career faculty members and on conducting tenure evaluations that are both thoughtful and fair. Sorcinelli's *Principles of Good Practice* (2000), which was sponsored by the American Association for Higher Education, offers ten principles of good practice, inventories to prompt academic leaders to examine their individual and institutional practices, and examples of concrete and innovative approaches from a variety of institutional settings. *Good Practice in Tenure Evaluation* (2000), a joint project of the American Council on Education, the American Association of University Professors, and the United Educators Association, provides additional advice for tenured faculty members, department chairs, and academic administrators regarding standards and procedures for tenure evaluation. In addition, institutions such as Kansas State University and professional and disciplinary associations such as the American Council on Education and the Modern Language Association sponsor annual and occasional seminars for department chairs. These programs focus on helping department chairs and other decision makers support the development of new faculty members and rethink traditional notions of faculty work in ways that begin to acknowledge varied ways of being a scholar.

Innovative Tenure and Promotion Statements

Perhaps one of the most exciting outcomes of *Scholarship Reconsidered* has been the enlarged view of scholarly work, as evidenced in new tenure and promotion policies at a number of colleges and universities. Various campuses have reviewed and rewritten policies to better capture and recognize the contributions of early-career and senior faculty members across the four scholarships. For example, Clemson University has installed an electronic faculty reporting system to address concerns about faculty roles and rewards. The system recognizes the need to redefine scholarship and it links faculty evaluation to established university goals. Every college now funds public service and outreach activities, which are part of the evaluation criteria. California State University–Long Beach has developed a new retention, tenure, and promotion policy emphasizing career-long professional development. The policy enlarges the dimensions considered in evaluating scholarship, and it strengthens the peer review of faculty work. The Associated New American Colleges is developing improved policies and practices in a number of areas of faculty work, such as workload differentiation, unit accountability, rewards, institutional service, faculty career stages, and faculty development. Following a needs assessment, working groups are meeting to outline both a vision and an agenda that will begin to incorporate and validate more varied ways of being a scholar, teacher, and institutional citizen.

Conclusion

Over the last decade, *Scholarship Reconsidered* has been widely discussed and has generated a range of policies, practices, and resources for improving the reward structure in general and the tenure process in particular. At the same time, studies of aspiring and new faculty members have identified the current tenure review process as a continuing obstacle to the full realization of a broader conceptualization of scholarly work. In order to move forward, we will need to both improve the tenure process as we now know it and create a new vision for the academy (Trower, Austin, and Sorcinelli, 2001). In the short term, within the confines of the current tenure system, we need to continue to support a broader conceptualization of the scholarly work of early-career faculty members. The aforementioned examples provide us with a starting point for communicating clear performance expectations for a range of scholarly work (throughout graduate school and the probationary years), ensuring orientation, mentoring, and feedback, offering flexibility and choice among various forms of scholarly work (and career tracks), and affording support for ongoing self-reflection and dialogue with colleagues about the kind of work and life we want to have.

Over the longer term, we have a wonderful opportunity to further transform our conceptions of faculty work and of the academy itself. A decade ago, in *Scholarship Reconsidered,* Boyer began the search for a new paradigm of faculty work that could meet the diverse and changing needs of our society. In response, colleges and universities have tested a range of new policies and practices that have enlarged our view of scholarly work and have directly addressed the tenure and promotion process. We now need to both institutionalize our best ideas and further articulate possible futures for the academy that ensure the health and livelihood of its faculty, especially its newest generation. The fresh approaches to faculty work generated by the varied and interrelated forms of scholarship proposed in Boyer's *Scholarship Reconsidered* will be an important touchstone in this endeavor.

References

Boice, R. *The New Faculty Member.* San Francisco: Jossey-Bass, 1992.

Boyer, E. L. *Scholarship Reconsidered: Priorities of the Professoriate.* Princeton, N.J.: The Carnegie Foundation for the Advancement of Teaching, 1990.

"The Future of Tenure: Interview with Richard Chait." *The Department Chair,* 1999, *10*(2), 3–5.

Glassick, C., Huber, M. T., and Maeroff, G. I. *Scholarship Assessed: Evaluation of the Professoriate.* San Francisco: Jossey-Bass, 1997.

Good Practice in Tenure Evaluation: Advice for Tenured Faculty, Department Chairs, and Academic Administrators. Washington, D.C.: American Council on Education, 2000.

Hutchings, P. *Making Teaching Community Property.* Washington, D.C.: American Association for Higher Education, 1996.

Hutchings, P., and Shulman, L. S. "The Scholarship of Teaching: New Elaborations, New Developments." *Change,* 1999, *31*(5), 11–15.

Menges, R. J., and Associates. *Faculty in New Jobs.* San Francisco: Jossey-Bass, 1999.
Mues, F., and Sorcinelli, M. D. *Preparing a Teaching Portfolio.* University of Massachusetts, Amherst, Center for Teaching, 2000.
Rice, R. E. *Making a Place for the New American Scholar.* Washington, D.C.: American Association for Higher Education, 1996.
Rice, R. E., Sorcinelli, M. D., and Austin, A. E. *Heeding New Voices.* Washington, D.C.: New Pathways Working Paper Series, 2000.
Sorcinelli, M. D. *Principles of Good Practice: Supporting Early-Career Faculty.* Washington, D.C.: American Association for Higher Education, 2000.
Sorcinelli, M. D., and Austin, A. E. *Developing New and Junior Faculty.* New Directions for Teaching and Learning, no. 50. San Francisco: Jossey-Bass, 1992.
Tice, S. L., Gaff, J. G., and Pruitt-Logan, A. S. "Preparing Future Faculty Programs: Beyond TA Development." In M. Marincovich, J. Prostco, and F. Stout (eds.), *The Professional Development of Graduate Teaching Assistants: The Practitioner's Handbook.* Bolton, Mass.: Anker Publishing, 1998.
Tierney, W. G., and Bensimon, E. M. *Promotion and Tenure: Community and Socialization in Academe.* Albany, N.Y.: State University of New York Press, 1996.
Trower, C. A. The Faculty Recruitment Study. *The Department Chair,* 2001, *11*(3), 4–5.
Trower, C. A., Austin, A. E., and Sorcinelli, M. D. "Paradise Lost: How the Academy Converts Enthusiastic Recruits into Early Career Doubters." *AAHE Bulletin,* 2001, *53*(9), 3–6.

MARY DEANE SORCINELLI is associate provost and director of the Center for Teaching at the University of Massachusetts and is an associate professor in the Department of Educational Policy, Research, and Administration.

5

Transforming the department into a team of people who support and trust each other not only revitalizes faculty members as their value is affirmed but also increases their contributions to the department and institution.

Engendering Trust Through Institutional Policies and Practices

Ann F. Lucas

Many faculty members in higher education feel disenfranchised because they are not engaged in scholarship. They feel shunned by their colleagues as unproductive members of the faculty and are often referred to as "the deadwood in the department." My consulting visits to 180 institutions in the last decade suggest that, for both senior and new faculty members, poor morale is almost palpable. "The rules of the game have changed," many senior faculty members say. One professor commented, "When I was hired, excellence in teaching was valued. Now, you are written off unless you are a productive scholar. Don't all of those years of high-quality teaching and working closely with students count for anything? I'll just put in my time until I am ready to retire."

During the year 2000, 50 percent of the full-time faculty were over age fifty-five and 68 percent were over fifty (National Center for Education Statistics, 1993). Academic chairs need to know how to create an environment that motivates such faculty members. Only 40 percent of 4,500 self-reporting academic chairs indicated that they have succeeded in motivating mid-career stagnant faculty members (Lucas, 1994). Most of these individuals can be productive scholars if institutions create an environment in which senior faculty members can maintain vitality and avoid burnout (Bland and Berquist, 1997).

The other group of unhappy faculty members are those on the tenure track who are uncertain as to what they need to do to secure tenure and promotion. After twenty-five years of practice as a faculty developer, Robert Boice (1992) has written, "As a rule, new faculty on our campuses are neglected resources whose development proceeds haphazardly. . . . Support programs for new faculty make sense as institutional investments; the costs, both economic and human, of losing new hires to competitors or to unproductive and unhappy beginnings are clearly greater than those of setting up effective support programs" (p. xi). Others, describing the plight and bewilderment of new faculty members as they try to determine what is expected of them to achieve tenure and promotion, are publishing research that indicates how institutional practices can turn enthusiastic new faculty members into early-career skeptics (Rice, Sorcinelli, and Austin, 2000; Sorcinelli, Austin, and Trower, 2001). Valuable advice on such topics as recruitment, mentoring, and evaluation during the tenure process provides institutions with survival techniques for new faculty members (Boice, 2000; Menges and Associates, 1999; Wunsch, 1994).

Changing the Culture to Value Faculty

To devalue individuals who have given lives of teaching and service to a college or university is unfair. Equally unjust is the lack of guidance of new faculty members regarding what is expected of them in order to achieve tenure.

Based on the redefinition of scholarship (Boyer, 1990; Rice, 1991), Robert M. Diamond, in Chapter Seven of this volume, has discussed the standards developed by more than a dozen of the national disciplinary and scholarly organizations for work to be considered scholarly engagement (Diamond and Adam, 1995). He also refers to the qualitative standards described in detail by Glassick, Huber, and Maeroff (1997) that will provide additional help in the personnel process for promotion and tenure committees, chairs, and deans.

For senior faculty members who have not published in some time, these two sets of guidelines make it easier to reframe some of the work they have been doing so that it fits the broader definition of scholarship. But there are particular changes in the department, college, and university structure that will make it easier for faculty members to initiate scholarly work and regain their self-esteem.

Departmental Practices That Make Scholarship Possible

Affirming the value of the faculty must begin in the department, which can engender trust as it implements institutional policies and practices. And the way departments function must be changed as they move from "tinkering to transformation" (Angelo, 2000).

Transform the Department into a Team. Transforming the department into a team is the best foundation on which trust between colleagues can be built. However, because faculty members have usually been trained to work independently rather than as team leaders or team members, a chair may feel that turning department members into a team is an overwhelming task.

So where does one start to transform faculty members into a team? It is usually a good idea to begin with a team effectiveness questionnaire so that department colleagues can monitor the ways in which they function together. They can then savor the characteristics that make their group effective and ask themselves how they made this happen. Finally, they can look at the ways in which they function that provide opportunities for team development and then generate a series of implementation steps to achieve their goals. A comprehensive discussion of the characteristics of team effectiveness may be found in Lucas and Associates (2000).

When department members function as a team, individuals look forward to coming to the department each day, enjoy the accomplishments at department and committee meetings, and feel a synergy that reflects the value of the greater achievements that can come about when people build on each other's ideas. Morale and productivity are high. In departments in which faculty members function as an effective team, (1) colleagues trust and are supportive of each other, (2) individuals feel valued, (3) people listen to each other's point of view, (4) departmental decision making and goal setting are done in a participatory manner, (5) problem solving, rather than winning, is the basis for discussion, and (6) conflict is viewed as a creative tension that reflects each person's desire to do what is best for the department rather than serving as an opportunity to engage in personal attacks.

Revisit the Mission Statement. As the department comes together as a team, an early step in encouraging faculty scholarship begins with revisiting the department's mission statement. If a disciplinary definition of scholarship is not included in the mission and goals of the department, scholarly activity will not increase. I am reminded of an article with the compelling title "On the Folly of Rewarding A While Hoping for B" (Kerr, 1975). When there is no alignment between what individual faculty members do and whether they move forward the goals of the department, scholarly engagement will not be valued by those in the hierarchy who must make recommendations or decisions about whether a particular type of scholarship will be valued. For example, in a marketing department, one faculty member proudly documented a paper he had presented to the Sherlock Holmes Society. Since the paper did not require a high level of discipline-related expertise and would have no significance or impact—thereby falling short of two of the six widely accepted criteria for determining quality of scholarship (Diamond and Adam, 1995), it was determined that this work had nothing to do with marketing or moving forward the goals of the department. Therefore, the work was not deemed worthy of serious consideration in the promotion process.

Department colleagues need to spend a day revisiting the mission statement at least every two or three years. Disciplines change, and new issues surface as important topics to be explored. Faculty members are sometimes doing important work that is not valued because the outcome of that work is not included in the department's mission statement. For example, three faculty members in a management department were not given any release time for research, although most other faculty members were on a reduced teaching load. Two of these faculty members were doing legitimate research on public health management and one was publishing on leadership and management in higher education. After the department revisited its mission statement, several changes were incorporated, including a revision of the language to read "organizational research" instead of "industrial organizational research." Now the work of these three faculty members could be valued and they were given release time for work that was legitimately covered by the mission statement.

Write or Rewrite the Departmental Policy Statement. Whereas a mission statement is short, often no more than a page, a departmental policy statement is quite detailed. Before it is written, faculty members must become thoroughly familiar with college and university policy statements, employee handbooks, the recommendations of their national disciplinary organizations, and their union contracts (if the university is unionized). Once the departmental policy statement has been crafted, with input from the entire department, choice of specialization in which the department sees itself expanding becomes clear and provides guidelines for recruiting new faculty members, and the departmental policy statement informs faculty members of what is required to gain tenure and promotion.

Unless department faculty members periodically take the time to develop a departmental policy statement and clear it with the dean and perhaps also with an educational policy committee in the college, if one exists, the curriculum may become stagnant. Instead of offering cutting-edge courses, it may become a hodgepodge of individual faculty interests—what Knefelkamp (1990) characterizes as the "collective autobiography of the faculty" (p. 10). A departmental policy statement also provides direction and guidelines for those who are seeking tenure and promotion, because they can see clearly whether their teaching, service, and scholarship accomplish the direction that the department has agreed should be taken. It prevents chairs and department promotion and tenure committees from creating wedges between themselves and faculty members who have provided documents for personnel decisions. Whenever objectively written documents exist, it is far less likely that individuals will feel that they have been treated unfairly.

Build in Accountability for Release Time. The departmental policy document should also include how accountability will be satisfied for release time. In some departments, release time for scholarship is considered an entitlement. Deans sometimes complain that a toxic climate has been created because faculty members are tenured and therefore unmotivated. Faculty members may say that this is the way it has always been and that there is no reward for scholarly engagement—so why bother?

Two attribution processes are operating here. One is the fundamental attribution error, which states that when the performance of a faculty member is inadequate, academic administrators believe it is because of some internal characteristics of the individual. For example, deans and chairs may blame faculty members for being lazy and unmotivated because they are tenured, and since most faculty members are tenured, they believe nothing can be done to motivate them. However, deans and chairs may ignore the external factors that can change this behavior. As an illustration, if accountability for release time for scholarship is built into university and departmental policy, faculty members will know that scholarship is being rewarded by release time. Thus, it is likely that their scholarship productivity will increase.

The self-serving bias, which is the second attribution process, states that faculty members whose research and publication record does not meet expectations will blame external circumstances for low scholarly productivity. They will believe that release time is an entitlement, and faculty members will say, perhaps incorrectly, "Engagement in scholarship does not pay off in this institution." Based on awareness of these two attribution errors, we may conclude that when expectations and consequences are mutually agreed upon, much of the animosity and adversarial relationships between faculty members and administrators can be significantly reduced.

Create a "Stop the Clock" Tenure Policy. A related question is, how can a faculty member be treated fairly when he or she is assigned a responsibility that makes it impossible to achieve stated outcomes? The most egregious example is when the position of chair is offered to an untenured faculty member because senior faculty members have refused a role that is not attractive to them. At the end of their term of office, these assistant professors proudly indicate to the department promotion and tenure committees that they have served as chairs for three or four years. The committee's response is often, Yes, but what scholarly activities have you produced? Faculty members are frequently bewildered because they truly believed that serving long hours and handling chair duties are sufficient to earn tenure. Accomplishing some major task, such as learning and implementing an outcomes assessment process in preparation for a visit from an accrediting committee, can also become a deterrent to tenure because the criteria of scholarly productivity were not made clear in advance. A new baby, terminally ill parents, or the emotional problems of one's adolescent offspring also deserve consideration. One faculty member served on the union and on the negotiating team for a new contract. He was furious when he was not promoted to full professor after all of the time he had devoted to union activities and bringing about a contract that was widely accepted by both the faculty and the administration. Whether or not such activities will be valued for promotion in a given university must be spelled out and approved by the dean and provost. A "stop the tenure clock" clause describing the circumstances under which time is or is not counted toward tenure needs to be inserted into the departmental policy document.

Creating a Culture That Also Values Scholarship. In addition to creating a climate in the department that is humanitarian and supportive, increasing scholarly productivity has two dimensions that the chair needs to address. One focus of intervention, which can help all of the faculty, is changing the culture of the department so that increasing scholarship becomes the norm. A second focus of intervention, which is more attuned to the individual, provides help for faculty members who would like to publish because that is part of what they feel a faculty member does, but they don't quite know how to get started. What follows describes a process for enhancing scholarship that can be adapted to all institutions, including community colleges.

A serious change in the culture is most likely to occur when the dean makes it clear that scholarship is expected and will be rewarded. If there is a compelling reason for this, such as that an increase in documented scholarship is essential if a proposal for a new graduate program is to be approved, or when it is believed that accreditation by a disciplinary group is needed if a college is to improve its competitive position for students if they are to receive tuition reimbursement from employers, this should become part of the message. The criteria for scholarship must be defined, a rationale for judging the importance of an activity must be provided, standards must be developed, and an indication of how the work of faculty members will be documented must be clearly stated. Such a statement would need approval from a college educational policy committee to ensure some consistency of standards, it would then need approval from the dean, and, finally, the provost or vice president for academic affairs would need to approve it. A policy that requires that more faculty members become active scholars is most likely to be accepted by the faculty when there is an agreed-upon need.

Specific Interventions to Increase Scholarship. Many faculty members feel that one of their responsibilities as an academic is to write or produce but that they need some help in order to be productive as authors or to do creative work in art and design, dance, or music. At this point, it is the chair who is in the best position to provide the help that "would-be" producers need by generating a change in the culture of the department. What the chair needs to address is the process—not just the outcome—of moving from the place where individuals do not produce to a place where they are productive scholars. There are some concrete interventions a chair can use. As in all cultural change, a chair needs to enlist the backing of the informal leaders of the department so that their input and support can be developed before the chair presents plans to the entire department. It also helps to set a goal, such as increasing average productivity by 10 percent for the department. Some of the strategies that work are as follows:

- Begin or resurrect department colloquia.
- Establish a norm that encourages the department's faculty members to talk about their creative ideas, read drafts of colleagues' papers, and provide supportive feedback.
- Devote some colloquia to "ideas in progress" or simply to a germ of an idea.
- Provide a jump start by encouraging faculty members who are not publishing to collaborate with those who are.

- Share national, regional, or local "calls for proposals" for presentations at professional conferences.
- Provide travel money for faculty members to attend and present at regional conferences and then conduct a workshop upon their return.
- Discuss with department faculty members, and with the dean, changing views of scholarship.
- Provide department workshops on (1) the national disciplinary association's redefinition of scholarship (Diamond and Adam, 1995), (2) criteria for evaluating scholarly work (Diamond, 1993; Glassick, Huber, and Maeroff, 1997), (3) "writing blocks" (Boice, 1990), and (4) grantsmanship.

Use Goal Setting as a Motivator. The chair's role in goal setting is to make the process a dynamic one rather than a paper procedure. Locke and Latham (1990) have demonstrated that goal setting is a powerful intervention for increasing both the productivity and the satisfaction of individuals. This can be done by making goals specific and measurable. Let goals be those that faculty members themselves want to achieve, but push forward the goals of the department as well. This provides the greatest leverage for motivation. Be certain that the goals are moderately difficult. Goals that are too low are not motivating; those that are too high doom the goal setter to failure. Have faculty members set particular objectives that will be accomplished at specific dates. Finally, given each faculty member's particular track record, be certain that the goals are realistic.

For those who have not been productive in scholarly activities in the past, use questions to help them. Questions such as the following are particularly helpful: (1) What would contribute to your professional development during the next year? (2) What goals would you find intellectually and emotionally stimulating at this point in your career? (3) If this were the best of all possible worlds, and you could accomplish whatever goals you wanted, what would they be? (4) What were your goals, your dreams, when you began your career in higher education? (5) Have you achieved any of these goals, and if so, how? (6) Are some of the goals you haven't reached ones that you can achieve now? and (7) How can I help you do that?

Obviously, some highly productive people do not need such questions to motivate them. However, all of us value periodic affirmation of our accomplishments. Affirmation by chairs who are respected by their colleagues is a valued commodity. The chair's role is often to celebrate the good news with faculty members about their achievements. Midstream corrections are a valuable intervention for faculty members who need periodic monitoring. This means checking on progress at agreed-upon times so that faculty members who tend to procrastinate will be motivated to meet such deadlines. Also, chairs may become cheerleaders or they may modify goals for those who have run into some kind of problem.

Conclusion

Implementing suggestions from the preceding discussion, along with a review of information found in the literature cited in this chapter, can provide helpful insights for institutions in creating an environment that will increase scholarship. Central to this process is the transforming of the department into a team of people who trust and support each other. Such a change revitalizes senior faculty members, who will feel supported and valued rather than diminished. These approaches will also be very helpful to chairs as they socialize new faculty members to become effective and productive members of the department. When scholarly productivity across the department increases, faculty members feel proud of what they, individually and together, are accomplishing. The institution, the department, the chair, and the faculty all emerge as winners.

References

Angelo, T. A. "Transforming Departments into Productive Learning Communities." In A. F. Lucas and Associates, *Leading Academic Change: Essential Roles for Department Chairs.* San Francisco: Jossey-Bass, 2000.

Bland, C. J., and Berquist, W. H. *The Vitality of Senior Faculty Members: Snow on the Roof—Fire in the Furnace.* ASHE-ERIC Higher Education Report, Volume 25, No. 7. Washington, D.C.: The George Washington University, Graduate School of Education and Human Development, 1997.

Boice, R. *Professors as Writers: A Self-Help Guide to Productive Writing.* Stillwater, Okla.: New Forums Press, 1990.

Boice, R. *The New Faculty Member.* San Francisco: Jossey-Bass, 1992.

Boice, R. *Advice for New Faculty Members.* Needham Heights, Mass.: Allyn & Bacon, 2000.

Boyer, E. L. *Scholarship Reconsidered: Priorities for the Professoriate.* Princeton, N.J.: The Carnegie Foundation for the Advancement of Teaching, 1990.

Diamond, R. M. "Changing Priorities and the Faculty Reward System." In R. M. Diamond and B. E. Adam (eds.), *Recognizing Faculty Work: Reward Systems for the Year 2000.* New Directions for Higher Education, no. 81. San Francisco: Jossey-Bass, 1993.

Diamond, R. M., and Adam, B. E. (eds.) *The Disciplines Speak: Rewarding the Scholarly, Professional, and Creative Work of Faculty.* Washington, D.C.: American Association for Higher Education, 1995.

Glassick, C. E., Huber, M. T., and Maeroff, G. I. *Scholarship Assessed: Evaluation of the Professoriate.* San Francisco: Jossey-Bass, 1997.

Kerr, S. "On the Folly of Rewarding A While Hoping for B." *Academy of Management Journal,* 1975, 18(4), 769–783.

Knefelkamp, L. "Seasons of Academic Life: Honoring Our Collective Autobiographies." *Liberal Education,* 1990, 76(3), 4–11.

Locke, E. A., and Latham, G. P. *A Theory of Goal Setting and Task Performance.* Englewood Cliffs, N.J.: Prentice Hall, 1990.

Lucas, A. F. *Strengthening Departmental Leadership: A Team-Building Guide for Chairs in Colleges and Universities.* San Francisco: Jossey-Bass, 1994.

Lucas, A. F., and Associates. *Leading Academic Change: Essential Roles for Department Chairs.* San Francisco: Jossey-Bass, 2000.

Menges, R. J., and Associates. *Faculty in New Jobs: A Guide to Settling in, Becoming Established, and Building Institutional Support.* San Francisco: Jossey-Bass, 1999.

National Center for Education Statistics. *"National Study of Postsecondary Faculty."* Washington, D.C.: U.S. Department of Education, Office of Educational Research and Improvement, 1993. (ED 375 792)

Rice, R. E. "The New American Scholar: Scholarship and the Purposes of the University." *Metropolitan Universities Journal,* 1991, *1*(4), 7–18.

Rice, R. E., Sorcinelli, M. D., and Austin, A. E. *Heeding New Voices: Academic Careers for a New Generation.* Washington, D.C.: Forum on Faculty Roles and Rewards, American Association for Higher Education, 2000.

Sorcinelli. M. D., Austin, A. E., and Trower, C. "Paradise Lost: How the Academy Converts Enthusiastic Recruits into Early-Career Doubters." *The Ninth Annual AAHE Conference on Faculty Roles and Rewards: The Changing Professoriate, New Technologies, New Generation,* Tampa, Fla., 2001.

Wunsch, M. A. *Mentoring Revisited: Making an Impact on Individuals and Institutions.* New Directions for Teaching and Learning, no. 57. San Francisco: Jossey-Bass, 1994.

ANN F. LUCAS is professor emerita at Fairleigh Dickinson University and author of three books and more than fifty articles and chapters on chair leadership.

6

Higher education in the twenty-first century calls for a paradigm shift in scholarship—a new approach that encourages academicians to consider not only the current practice and product of research at their institutions but also the well-being of the practitioners—in short, to explore the soul of scholarship.

The Soul of Scholarship

Kina S. Mallard

If scholarship had a soul, how would that change the way we value research? The traditional approach to evaluating faculty scholarship has been to count the number of academic publications and presentations while considering the importance of the journal or conference. There is some merit in this quantitative emphasis, because a university's reputation and ability to acquire grants and funding for research is often based on statistical information. However, considering the result of scholarship is but one way to determine a faculty member's value; it is not the only way. In fact, one could question whether this approach has been successful in increasing scholarly productivity.

In a 1989 Higher Education Research Institute survey, over half the faculty members surveyed had written nothing professionally in the past two years, and in their overall career over 30 percent had never published an article. According to a 1992 editorial in the *Chronicle of Higher Education,* 55 percent of faculty members had never published a book, 22 percent had never published in a professional journal, and almost 30 percent were not engaged in scholarly research that would lead to publication. The figures probably have not changed appreciably since then. The fact is, most faculty members are not prolific researchers.

I believe we need a new approach to scholarship—a paradigm shift that focuses not so much on the product of research as on the person and the research process. Professors in the new millennium are looking for balance, community, understanding, and acceptance. Colleges and universities need to discover how to meet the professional development *and* personal needs of future scholars while maintaining high research standards.

This chapter seeks to challenge college and university leaders to maintain their research mandates and to increase the number of professors

NEW DIRECTIONS FOR TEACHING AND LEARNING, no. 90, Summer 2002 © Wiley Periodicals, Inc.

engaged in scholarship by considering scholar-development stages and developing scholar-mentoring programs, with the goal being the development of a community of dialogue. This approach is key to embracing a new value of scholarship—the soul.

Scholar-Development Stages

Scholar-development can be considered in stages, including establishment, advancement, maturation, and withdrawal. When administrators understand the motivation of faculty members at different stages of their careers, they can help develop challenging yet realistic research expectations.

The Establishment Stage. The establishment stage occurs when faculty members first begin teaching—most of them starting out when they are in their late twenties or early thirties. Some of those establishing a professional career before obtaining their advanced degree are in their mid- to late thirties or older. And so some beginning faculty members may be as young as twenty-five and some may be as old as fifty—but, regardless of age, many are novices when it comes to the challenges of teaching and scholarship.

The faculty member's greatest concern during the establishment stage is the need to acclimate quickly to his or her new environment. Part of this acclimation is learning to set priorities and manage time wisely. New faculty members are juggling the complex process of understanding academic life, preparing lectures, establishing their place in the department, grading papers, and maneuvering numerous other tasks. For ABD (All But Dissertation) faculty members, these tasks compete with and add pressure to the task of completing the dissertation, and for those with terminal degrees in hand, these responsibilities add to the strain of carving out enough time for writing and research.

In a study of new faculty members, Boice (1992) found that they tended to procrastinate. They tended to relegate research to a specific time period—usually summer vacation, during which there would be large blocks of uninterrupted time available to them. Yet, at the end of the summer vacation between their first and second years, they had produced an average of only 4.32 verified manuscript pages; by the end of their second year on campus, they had written an average of an additional 4.21 verified manuscript pages.

Productive scholars report that their success depends on scheduled amounts of dedicated scholarship time. Devoting one to two hours daily to research and writing seemed to be a better success strategy than hoping for large blocks of time in the summer. Boice (1992) concluded that new faculty members who can find as little as an hour per weekday to write generally manage to submit about 1.5 manuscripts per year—an output level consistent with the expectations of tenure and promotion committees at most campuses. His research further reveals that faculty members adopting a schedule of brief daily periods for writing experience less busyness and stressfulness during their first few years on campus.

The challenge of acclimation and anxiety about new roles calls for a strong mentor. Although new faculty members need the encouragement of their department chair—and the chair certainly should fill that role, the chair can also be perceived as intimidating by new faculty members. After all, it was the chair who looked over her glasses and said, "Now, you're *sure* you can have that dissertation finished within your first year at the university?" Therefore, the chair may not be the best mentor at this time. But senior faculty members—those in the maturation and withdrawal stages—make excellent mentors for establishment-stage faculty members. In addition to finding mentors on campus, new professors should seek relationships within their professional organizations. Furthermore, chairs and department colleagues can encourage new faculty members to continue graduate school relationships and become involved in state, regional, and national organizations.

Once the dissertation is completed, new faculty members may need a respite from scholarship, but it is important that the hiatus be brief. Academic departments are filled with seasoned professors lamenting their rusty research skills. The postdissertation period of the establishment stage can be very exciting for the new professor. During the second or third year of teaching, the professor hits a certain stride, where things begin to run as smoothly as can be expected in academic life. At this point, the young scholar needs to partner with others in the department or on campus who are interested in the same research ideas or trained in the same methodologies. A writing regimen that is both practical and productive should be established. Boice (1992) offers the following rule of balance: "At most, writing deserves to be a moderate priority, one that can be handled in brief daily sessions amid other, more important tasks. When practiced daily, writing stays freely in mind and requires little or no warm-up time. Perfectionism in writing is best indulged in final revisions, not in initial drafts. Productive writing is best undertaken as a leap of faith, before one feels ready. The most productive and cited writers, surprisingly, balance time spent on writing with that for collegiality and teaching" (pp. 170–171).

The transition from graduate school or other careers produces frustration as new faculty members seek to understand new expectations and a new culture. Adding to this frustration is concern about how much research and publication will be expected in order to gain tenure. Each institution has different standards, both written and assumed. Colleagues, chairs, and deans are in the best position to communicate the expectations as well as alert the new professor to research resources available on campus.

The novice scholar may not experience success at first, and colleagues should resist the appearance of arrogance by touting only the elite journals and conferences. Sharing the soul of scholarship involves helping the scholar find the best scholarly fit. Some establishment faculty members are ready for top journals and national conferences, but others, like my colleague Steve, need to experience success at the state level before becoming confident enough to submit their work to regional conferences. Many professional disciplines have state conferences that provide excellent opportunities for new scholars to share research ideas, deliver papers in a supportive environment, and receive advice from more seasoned professors.

The Advancement Stage. Faculty members with a little experience under their belt have moved into the advancement stage. Advancement usually occurs between year three and year seven of academic service; however, the advancement period will vary. At this stage, faculty members have reached a certain comfort level in the classroom and are discovering their research strengths. These professors are usually independent contributors and autonomous performers who are beginning to clarify long-term career options.

Peer relationships become important during advancement and therefore administrators are relied on less frequently for guidance. Faculty members are developing their own performance goals in teaching and research, administrators and faculty members need to be on the same page in terms of promotion and tenure requirements, and chairs and colleagues should help their new colleagues understand the expectations of the department and the university. Most deans and department chairs will say that they are interested in quality, not quantity, but a quick perusal of their promotion and tenure standards will reveal quantitative, not qualitative, measurements. As cynics in the academic profession frequently lament, "Our dean can't read, but he can count."

Successful scholars look beyond their institution's research expectations and strive to meet their discipline's standards as well. Because defining publishing productivity varies among disciplines, chairs, faculty development personnel, and colleagues can help the advancing scholar interpret these standards. For example, the field of journalism and mass communications is concerned with number of publications, while accountants limit their standards to publications in journal articles. Boyer (1990) writes:

> There is, in most disciplines, a fairly clear hierarchy of journals and a recognized process of peer review. . . . For example, a department chairman at a ranking research university reported that "in psychology, all that counts is articles in high prestige journals. Even books don't count as much." Another scholar stated, "Economists have carefully studied publications and have developed a rank order for them. At research institutions, one must publish in particular journals. Quantitative studies are better than qualitative studies." Another scholar told our researcher, "Books are more important than articles at the Harvard Business School. And the book must get good reviews" [p. 29].

Just as the establishment stage is colored by the completion of the dissertation, the advancement stage is a race toward tenure. The faculty member wishes to attain some kind of meaningful achievement and is painfully conscious of the kinds of scholarship respected by his institution. Even in colleges and universities whose mission is primarily teaching, research expectations are growing. Faculty members at most four-year institutions feel some pressure to demonstrate scholarship. One professor expressed his frustration to me during an informal coffee session: "Once I had the dissertation behind me I thought it would be easy, but I'm not sure where to go from here. I followed the advice of one of my doctoral professors and made a file titled 'Future Research Projects.' Now I have a file with a lot of great ideas, but I am lost as to where to start. I need someone to help me focus, to help me find direction."

Faculty members during this stage must receive help focusing or they will lose the research momentum they had while working on their dissertation. During this period, colleagues, department chairs, and faculty development centers can help the professor determine what kind of scholarship he or she wants to pursue. Recently, a professor came by our Center for Faculty Development to talk with me about publishing. Feeling somewhat pressured by the new emphasis on scholarship in her department, she shared with me how she had been hired because of her professional experience—to teach practical applications of her content area and not to produce scholarship. As we talked I realized that producing scholarship for a refereed journal was beyond her skills and desire. Her passion was clearly for helping teachers improve their teaching. I asked her about trade publications for practicing teachers and she brought a few to my office. As we looked through them together, a light bulb went on. "I could write these kinds of articles," she said. She had found her niche, a place where she could be successful and make a difference in her profession. At some institutions, these applied articles might not be counted as scholarship; however, I hope that the academy will see the emergence of a broader acceptance and increased value of different kinds of contributions to the academic disciplines.

It is critical at the advancement stage for the professor to make some progress in the area of scholarship. If the faculty member isn't progressing, the chair or mentor should attempt to clarify the reasons for lack of performance. Reasons may vary, but lack of effective research skills, spending an inordinate amount of time on teaching, inability to prioritize tasks, and lack of funding are common reasons for prolonging research efforts.

The Maturation Stage. The third stage of career development is maturation. During this period, usually posttenure, the faculty member reaches a plateau. He or she may hold onto career successes and help less experienced colleagues. However, dissatisfaction could start to set in during this period and the faculty member may need redirection and new challenges. It is important that mature faculty members not be dismissed; they still have many good, productive years left.

Maturation can be the most rewarding phase for academicians. By this time, professors have a clear focus on the kind of scholarship that best fits their education and interests, have had some success with presentations or publications, and have research goals mapped out for the future. The mid-career scholar is often the most prolific and carries tremendous influence in the department and university. Because of the awareness of the pending stage—withdrawal—the maturing professors seek balance between career and family and at the same time have confidence in their abilities and contributions to their discipline.

Although this stage is the most rewarding, it can also be extremely frustrating for many scholars. During the maturation stage, faculty members become keenly aware of their shortcomings. They tend to compare themselves with the "stars" of the institution or of their discipline and may not feel up to standard. Boyer (1990) writes, "It is unrealistic to expect all faculty members, regardless of their interests, to engage in research and to publish on a regular timetable. For most scholars, creativity simply doesn't work that way" (p. 27). Most professors publish very few articles but may involve themselves in scholarship by giving presentations and by being active in professional organizations.

Interestingly, new faculty members can help jump-start the research productivity of seasoned faculty members and prevent mid-career professors from retiring from scholarship prematurely. Recently a new faculty member joined the education department at my university, and her dissertation was on a topic that was related to the research of a senior faculty member. Once their similar interests were discovered, they applied for and received an internal research grant and embarked on a joint research project. Their work culminated in a presentation at a regional university that generated ideas for further research. And, as might be expected, establishment- and advancement-level faculty members, eager to learn the ropes and gain credibility in their professions, can benefit greatly when paired with elder faculty members. The synergy created by forty- or fifty-somethings working alongside twenty- or thirty-somethings can produce exemplary scholarship and can build close relationships.

Chairs, faculty development professionals, and peers can also play a critical role in identifying research support opportunities. Maturing faculty members will feel valued when they are used in training, guiding, influencing, or directing others. Having self-confidence and good interpersonal skills, as well as learning to derive satisfaction from another's accomplishments, are necessary for successfully surviving this career stage.

The Withdrawal Stage. The final stage—withdrawal—marks the beginning of the end of the faculty member's career. During this stage, professors are preparing to leave. They may be letting go of organizational attachments while feeling a sense of accomplishment and fulfillment. These faculty members are confident of their positions and secure in their jobs. They have earned the right to be heard and therefore are in a position to make things happen.

Motivating faculty members who are withdrawing is a challenge. Although they may not be actively involved in research, most still enjoy sharing their research. Including them on scholarship panels and in small group research discussions is valuable both to their personal self-esteem and to their professional establishment and advancement. Because elder faculty members no longer feel the need to compete for funding, credibility, time, or other resources, they can help encourage younger scholars. Administrators can help them see that working with other professors and sharing their past research adds to the legacy they will leave behind.

Although posttenured, preretirement faculty members are sometimes seen as doing little more than showing up to teach classes, the reality is that many faculty members in the withdrawal stage have not yet thrown in the towel. Seasoned faculty members' analytical and problem-solving skills are usually very highly developed and thus they can share a mature perspective with the new scholar. Furthermore, their contacts can help the novice faculty member network in his or her field. Paired with energetic faculty members in their twenties and thirties, these seasoned professors can give their younger, less experienced colleagues perspective and can share wisdom from the trenches.

Success in each of the four scholar-development stages is dependent upon three key players: the department chair, who is in the best position to identify faculty strengths and weaknesses, the dean, who must be sensitive to workload and resource challenges, and faculty development personnel, who provide guidance, training, strategic research planning, and other forms of support to faculty members.

In the past, the academic life has been an isolated life. As we consider the soul of scholarship, we must consider the importance of collegiality. One way to help develop scholars while supporting collegiality is through scholar mentoring.

Scholar Mentoring and a Community of Dialogue

Parker Palmer, in *The Courage to Teach* (1998), talks about the culture of fear that permeates academic life. Faculty members, says Palmer, feel disconnected from one another, and the divisive nature created by the competitive race for research money, promotion, and tenure pits faculty member against faculty member. Rather than being a solitary, competitive activity, the best scholarship brings faculty members together and mutually reinforces their efforts in research and teaching. Faculty members, usually fiercely independent, must admit that they need each other when it comes to scholarly development. Establishing scholar-mentoring programs is one way to provide opportunities for faculty members to collaborate formally in their research efforts.

There is no definitive formula for nurturing and selecting scholar mentors, and a quick perusal of mentoring literature poses no clear model for what works. In addition, little has been written about academic scholarship mentoring, except in professor-student relationships. The key, then, is for each department or unit leader to consider carefully the people and process that best fit their culture.

The People. Scholar-mentoring relationships can happen spontaneously and can be informal in nature. This is the most productive and beneficial way for mentoring to take place; however, administrators often have to help the process, and having a formally structured mentoring program in place is critical. The chair, dean, or anyone responsible for faculty development can select research mentors. Because scholar mentors will be a new concept to many, it is wise to hand-select the first group of participants and invite them to an informational meeting to discuss the purpose and expectations.

The pairing of scholar mentors with their mentorees—younger, less experienced colleagues—is challenging and must be carefully considered. It may be difficult to pair faculty members with similar interests for long-term relationships, especially at smaller colleges where there may be only one Russian literature or media effects scholar. If this is the case, professors should seek relationships within their professional organizations. Chairs and department colleagues can encourage new faculty members to continue graduate school relationships and become involved in state, regional, and national organizations.

Excellent scholar mentors can come from any of the four career stages; however, faculty members in the maturation and withdrawal stages have the most time to devote. They also do not have the added pressure of competing with their mentorees for institutional dollars. The best mentors are optimistic, encouraging, and straightforward. They have the best interests of their mentorees at heart and therefore are not shy about giving constructive criticism and helping faculty members find venues for their completed research.

The Process. Successful mentoring is an ongoing process and involves a strong commitment on the part of both the mentor and the mentoree. It is generally agreed that good mentoring includes a regular discussion of goals and expectations, flexibility that allows for different work styles and work schedules, and tangible measures of success or accomplishment. The responsibilities of the mentor can range from providing simple encouragement to participating as an equal partner in the research process. Ideally, the mentor should support quality research that leads the young scholar toward publication. The mentor can work with the mentoree to identify and acquire additional skills that will enhance the young scholar's ability to produce scholarship.

The successful mentor-scholar relationship will employ various approaches, including (1) visiting with the mentoree to discuss areas of interest, (2) encouraging the mentoree to publish from his or her dissertation, (3) helping the mentoree explore different possibilities for presentations and publications in his or her field and matching his or her style to the various publications, (4) discussing with the mentoree how to rewrite conference papers into journal articles and how to identify appropriate journals in the field for publication, (5) helping the mentoree perfect the craft of submitting abstracts for presentations, (6) encouraging the mentoree to submit work to state, regional, and national conferences, (7) developing learning circles to explore grant opportunities, (8) sharing relevant articles and research with the mentoree, and (9) helping the mentoree develop strategies to build on his or her research.

Scholar mentors can also help their mentorees with task management. A common complaint in academe is not having enough time to do research. I remember a conversation I had with my mentor, Dr. Faye Julian, dean of undergraduate academic affairs at the University of Tennessee. We were talking at a professional conference and I lamented the lack of time to do research. Fresh from completing my Ph.D., I had accepted a chair position and for two years had poured myself into the administrative tasks needed for my job. I knew my research skills were getting rusty but didn't see how I could fit one more thing into my day. She replied with great wisdom, "Kina, write about what you *do*. Write about being a department chair." As a result of her encouragement, I combined my theoretical knowledge of communication theory with my practical experience as chair of the communication arts department and began writing for *The Department Chair Newsletter* and similar publications.

Administrators and faculty developers can help nurture mentors and mentorees by providing opportunities for the pairs to share their experiences in public forums. Some scholar-mentoring programs will result in joint research projects, whereas others will help faculty members build relationships and respect for different research topics and research methods. Stipends for scholar mentors can provide incentive for recruiting new mentors, but the motivation for continuing as a mentor will come from within.

Community of Dialogue. Whereas scholar mentoring is a formal way to pair together those with common research interests, the ideal situation would be the emergence of a community of dialogue. The new generation of scholars craves collaboration and community. Common academic lore that academic research is a solitary activity is not supported in the literature. Creswell (1985) found that the most productive and cited writers in academe spend as much time networking with colleagues as they do writing. A tenured art professor at Union University in Jackson, Tennessee, attended a faculty development session on scholarship and reminisced about his graduate school days. "I would get up in the morning and paint the entire day," he said. "Others who shared the studio with me made comments about my work and faculty were ready and willing to critique what I was doing. That's what I miss most about graduate school—*the community that helped me be productive.*"

Parker Palmer (1998) would most likely understand the meaning in that faculty member's reflection—and perhaps we all do. In order to discover the soul of scholarship, professors need a community that encourages the kind of productivity that comes from formal and informal faculty interaction. I envision a community where dialogue is prevalent, energizing, and productive. I experienced this community while writing this chapter. I discussed the concept of soul informally with my Christian studies colleagues and offered my writing to a communications professor within my discipline and a history colleague outside my discipline for formal criticism. Their comments and suggestions motivated me to revise, refine, and rethink. This chapter is stronger as a result of the respect and trust my colleagues and I share. A spirit of helpfulness and collaboration is imperative for creating a community of dialogue.

Strategies for Putting the Soul into Scholarship

To understand and practice the soul of scholarship, academicians need a paradigm shift. We need to come down from our lofty perches in our ivory towers and reach out to our colleagues. I offer three strategies to guide campus leaders in changing their department, school, and university culture.

1. *Foster collaboration, not competition.* Resources in higher education are scarce. Only a handful of scholars will receive competitive grants, be chosen for coveted release time to write, achieve entry into the top journals in their field, or be recognized nationally for their work. There are never enough resources to go around, and good scholars don't always receive the rewards they have earned. Competition is inevitable, but leaders can work hard to squelch the ills of jealousy and competition. To foster a culture of collaboration, administrators can earmark some research money for collaborative projects, some large development funds can be divided into smaller awards so that more faculty members can take advantage of them, and departments can hold colloquia for their majors, where faculty members can work together to plan and share research projects.

2. *Strive to encourage, not discourage.* Academicians sometimes have a propensity for being critical and cynical. Reaching for the soul of scholarship means intentionally looking for opportunities to encourage your colleagues. Constructive criticism is valuable when asked for and given appropriately, but, when unsolicited, it halts research productivity. Look for opportunities to ask colleagues how their research is progressing, send notes or e-mail messages when you read about a publication or presentation they have given, and offer suggestions when prompted. The act of encouragement takes little time and is free. It does take some energy on the part of the encourager, but it increases energy for the encouraged.

3. *Value diversity, not dissension.* Research in the academy can vary as much as the individual personalities of the professors. My research

looks very different from that of the theater professor in my department, and my university's definition of scholarship may be quite different from that of other universities. It is easy for scholars in different disciplines to lapse into criticism and create dissension among colleagues. Much of this criticism is based on a lack of understanding of different fields of study. Faculty development personnel and deans can provide both formal and informal opportunities for scholars to share their research with each other. Interdepartmental and cross-campus learning communities can also be established to discuss research and to develop research goals.

Conclusion

A new value in scholarship is to envision, honor, celebrate, and relate to the whole being of scholars—not only to their minds but also to their souls, not only to their reasoning but also to their passion, not only to their dossiers but also to their dreams. And as we relate to these scholars as individuals and sensitively consider their career stages, we bring them together in community with an emphasis on scholar-mentoring programs and venues for scholarship sharing. This community of scholars will then work together, establishing research principles, programs, and processes that reflect an interest in the people behind the product—the soul behind the scholarship.

References

Boice, R. *The New Faculty Member: Supporting and Fostering Professional Development.* San Francisco: Jossey-Bass, 1992.

Boyer, E. L. *Scholarship Reconsidered: Priorities of the Professoriate.* Princeton, N.J.: The Carnegie Foundation for the Advancement of Teaching, 1990.

Creswell, J. W. *Faculty Research Performance: Lessons from the Sciences and Social Sciences.* ASHE-ERIC Higher Education Reports. Washington, D.C.: The George Washington University Press, 1985.

McCaughey, R. A. "Why Research and Teaching Can Coexist." *Chronicle of Higher Education,* Aug. 5, 1992, p. A36.

Palmer, P. J. *The Courage to Teach.* San Francisco: Jossey-Bass, 1998.

KINA S. MALLARD is director of the Center for Faculty Development and chair of the communication arts department at Union University in Jackson, Tennessee.

PART THREE

New Visions

Many factors determine the definition of scholarship at any given time, including the discipline, the priorities of the institution and academic unit, and the interests of the individual. This chapter discusses these influences, traces recent developments in how we view the scholarly role of faculty members, and it recommends an institutional approach for bringing fairness and quality into faculty reward systems.

Defining Scholarship for the Twenty-First Century

Robert M. Diamond

For the greater part of the twentieth century, most professors paid little attention to defining the term "scholarship" or to addressing what was meant by "scholarly work." Most individuals and disciplines bought into the concept growing out of the sciences that to be scholarly an activity needed to be "original" research that led to publication as a book or an article in one of the more significant discipline-based, refereed journals.

As the century progressed, however, less attention was paid to the importance or impact of the work and more was given to where it appeared in print. Original research was emphasized, with little recognition given to application, teaching, creative work, or professional activities that might take place in "nontraditional" settings. The impact of this approach, while seldom mentioned publicly, was at times extremely unfortunate not only for individual faculty members but also for the disciplines themselves.

By the 1980s, faculty members who placed emphasis on teaching or service, or whose research was viewed as more applied than basic, often did so at great personal risk, jeopardizing tenure or sacrificing any hope of gaining full professorship.

There were, however, three independent initiatives that together were to bring the issue of what scholarship is and how it is defined to the consciousness of the academy: the work on the scholarship of professional service, led by Ernest Lynton, Sandra Elman, and Sue Marx Smock (1985), the redefinition of scholarship into four basic classifications, developed by Eugene Rice (1991), and built on by Ernest Boyer (1990), and the project I led (1997) at Syracuse University to describe scholarship in the various disciplines.

NEW DIRECTIONS FOR TEACHING AND LEARNING, no. 90, Summer 2002 © Wiley Periodicals, Inc.

In addition, a campuswide study at Syracuse to determine the perceptions of faculty members and administrators on the balance between teaching and research was to lead to a series of national studies that encompassed over 170 institutions and collected data from over forty-six thousand faculty members and academic administrators. This study was to show that most faculty members believed that the criteria used for tenure and promotion were "out of balance" with what they believed was important and appropriate for their institution, with this imbalance being most pronounced at research and doctoral-granting institutions. Although dissatisfaction varied in degree among disciplines, it was felt by all.

The Disciplines Address Scholarship

As part of the Syracuse Project, funds were received from several foundations to support establishing discipline-based task forces charged with developing statements that described more fully the work of the faculty members in their fields. The goal was to produce statements that were descriptive and not prescriptive and that would encourage academic departments to develop a priority system for faculty work that was appropriate for their own institution.

By the end of the century, statements had been developed, approved, and disseminated by members of over twenty-five disciplines. The full reports from most of the participating disciplines can be found in a two-volume set edited by Robert Diamond and Bronwyn Adam: *The Disciplines Speak* (1995) and *The Disciplines Speak II* (2000). Contributions from the arts, the humanities, the social and natural sciences, and professional programs are included in these collections—and additional statements are still being developed.

What the statements do show is that there are indeed major differences among the disciplines as to what faculty members do and what members of the different fields believe scholarly activity includes. From the comments of hundreds of faculty members in developing these statements and from their open-ended responses in the national study, it is also apparent that the views of faculty members are shaped by a number of forces: their discipline, the program from which they graduated, their own personal interests and priorities, and the climate and mission of the department and institution in which they work.

The diversity among disciplines, departments, and faculty members, and the significance of the faculty reward system's sensitivity to what activities constitute scholarly work, become very clear as one reads the disciplinary statements themselves.

At the End of the Twentieth Century

The move to improve the tenure and promotion system and to redefine and expand the definition of scholarly work will certainly be recognized as a major area of transition in higher education at the end of the twentieth

Figure 1. Scholarship and the Work of Faculty Members

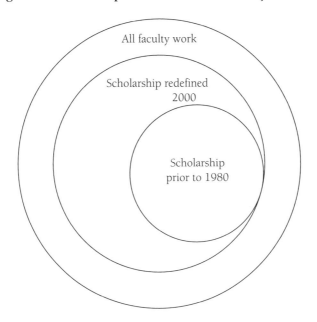

century. The topic has been placed on the agenda of most institutions, as well as that of the annual meeting of the American Association for Higher Education's Forum on Faculty Roles and Rewards, which is as large a convention as the association's National Conference on Higher Education. A 1991–1996 study (Diamond and Adam, 1997) shows that priorities, perceptions, and the faculty reward system itself were indeed changing at a number of institutions.

The definition of scholarly work in many disciplines now encompasses a larger proportion of the work that faculty members do than ever before (see Figure 1). However, the ramifications of these changes are still limited on a number of campuses.

The last decade has also seen the publication of a number of reference works aimed at assisting faculty members and administrators interested in developing a faculty reward system that is sensitive to the needs of the institution while recognizing the differences among the disciplines and the individual strengths of faculty members. Two recent publications describe the contents and source of policy statements from the full range of institutions (Trower, 2000; Diamond, 1999).

Much has been accomplished, but the impact of these initiatives on individuals and institutions varies considerably. Some disciplines have developed comprehensive and truly landmark publications, whereas others have not. At some institutions there have been systemic changes in the process and criteria used in the faculty reward system, whereas at others the system that was in place in 1950 is still functioning today, and some institutions are becoming even narrower in their approach.

For some faculty members and administrators, the chance to broaden the range of activities considered scholarly represents an opportunity; for others, it is a threat. There is particular concern among faculty members who themselves are quite comfortable with the research-based approach to scholarship and who see any attempt to broaden the scope of activities considered scholarly as having the potential for diminishing their power and resources—a "zero-sum game" perspective. Some administrators and faculty members also see any effort to increase the importance of applied research, teaching, and service as having the potential for reducing the prestige of their institution or their programs, and for some, image is the primary concern.

There is also a growing tug-of-war on many campuses between the professional schools and the arts and sciences. The arts and sciences have seen a reduction in the number of majors, particularly at the graduate level, but many of the professional schools face major enrollment increases. As a result, some programs need more resources to cover classes and the services they are being asked to provide, whereas others are attempting to place greater importance on research and on the reduction of class size and teaching loads.

The impact of these trends on the very structure and politics of institutions cannot be underestimated. Any change can be difficult, challenging, and discomfiting. When fundamental values and long-standing traditions are affected, as they will be, the process will not be easy; we can expect extensive debate and a great deal of heat. Financial stress, a major increase in the number of high school graduates entering postsecondary education, and increased competition will only add fuel to this mix in the years ahead.

Scholarship for the Twenty-First Century

Any attempt to define scholarship within a particular context of faculty work is doomed to failure. Some disciplines are more comfortable with a research/publication basis for scholarly work than others are, but in every academic field there are problems with this approach. In the Syracuse study, for example, every discipline reported that some significant activities of faculty members, although scholarly in nature, did not quite fit the research/publication paradigm. Some disciplines' task forces went so far as to recommend that the term "scholarship" itself not be used and that it be replaced by "the creative work of faculty," or, in the case of business and management, the "professional work of faculty."

And yet the academy does need a definitional "coin of the realm," a way of describing the scholarly aspects of faculty work that can be used across the disciplines and departments and among institutions. To meet this need, we propose to look not at the activity or where it takes place but at the common characteristics of any work that make it a scholarly enterprise.

In addition, as Eugene Rice (1996) notes, the results of scholarship must be public: "The established view of scholarship has another strength that needs to be built into a new broader approach. Research is shared and is public. It energizes [the] faculty because it has the potential for being not only extrinsically but [also] intrinsically rewarding. It is grounded in an associational life that opens the possibilities of a community of discourse tied directly to one's own intellectual interest and expertise. It is also a cosmopolitan activity that is not only public but [also] portable. Achievements are recognized, rewarded by peers, documented, and available to others for evaluation" (p. 13).

To do this, we build upon two earlier publications: Chapter One in Diamond and Adam's *Recognizing Faculty Work* (1993) and Glassick, Huber, and Maeroff's *Scholarship Assessed* (1997).

Whereas Diamond and Adam's work with disciplinary association task forces has led to describing a set of conditions that characterize the *products* of scholarly, professional, and creative work (1993), Glassick, Huber, and Maeroff (1997) focused more on the *process* of scholarship itself. It is perhaps a combination of these two elements—product and process—that will provide us with a practical and functional way of evaluating the scholarly work of faculty members. This approach would eliminate many of the problems we now face as faculty members and administrators when we are placed in positions where we must evaluate the scholarship of another faculty member.

If, as institutional policy, we focus more on the qualities that make an activity scholarly and less on the specific activity itself, there are a number of advantages.

- Individual academic units can be given the responsibility of determining *if* a specific activity falls within the work of the discipline and the priorities of the institution, school, college, and department.
- The criteria that are used can be clear, easy to understand, and consistent across all disciplines, thus reducing problems for administrators, committees, and the faculty members being reviewed.
- The system is fair and the criteria are clearly understood, with no one discipline or group of disciplines determining what scholarship should be for another discipline or group of disciplines.
- The process is cost-effective, in that faculty members up for review know what is required of them and faculty members serving on review committees can focus their attention on the quality of the product and process rather than on whether or not the activity should be considered scholarly.

In addition, this approach eliminates the need to place the activity itself in a specific category. Although what a faculty member does may represent basic or applied research—be it in the context of teaching, service, or the

Table 1. Criteria for Considering an Activity Scholarly

1. The activity or work requires a high level of discipline-related expertise.
2. The activity or work is conducted in a scholarly manner with
   - clear goals
   - adequate preparation
   - appropriate methodology
3. The activity or work and its results are appropriately and effectively documented and disseminated. This reporting should include a reflective critique that addresses the significance of the work, the process that was used, and what was learned.
4. The activity or work has significance beyond the individual context. It
   - breaks new ground or is innovative
   - can be replicated or elaborated
5. The activity or work, both process and product or result, is reviewed and judged to be meritorious and significant by a panel of one's peers.

It will be the responsibility of the academic unit to determine if the activity or work itself falls within the priorities of the department, school or college, discipline, and institution.

creative arts—the setting is not of prime importance. What is most important is that the process that is followed—as well as the results that are obtained—represents a high level of scholarship supported by appropriate documentation.

A recommendation for the structure and context of a policy statement will be found in Table 1. Designed as a starting point for discussion, this approach will ideally serve as the basis for an institutional statement on scholarship. This initial statement is then expanded upon as the focus moves from the institutional statement to the school and college statement, and then to the departmental policy and guidelines for faculty roles and rewards.

As previously noted, it is the role of the academic unit or department to identify those specific "areas of work" that fall within the priorities of the department, within the context of the discipline, and within the mission and vision of the institution.

In the next few decades, we can expect to see major changes in the role faculty members play and in what they are asked to do. As institutions face increased competition from the for-profit sector and from other institutions, as the arts and sciences are asked to rethink what a basic core program for all students should look like, as there are increased calls for assessment and accountability, and as there are increased demands for faculty members to become more involved in their communities, how most faculty members spend their time will change significantly. As a direct result of technology and of what we know about teaching and learning, we can also expect major changes not only in the roles of the student and the teacher but also in the structure of academic programs themselves. There will be demands for new academic programs and for existing programs to be modified or eliminated.

And in every one of these initiatives, faculty members must play a central part. In addition, we can expect to see a continued blending of disciplines and an increased involvement of faculty members in projects where they are part of a team. Faculty members may find that as a result of all these pressures, institutions will play a far greater role than ever before in determining priorities and in identifying where time should be spent and what scholarly work should be supported.

Much will change as a result of all of these forces, but the faculty reward system that is in place on campuses must also be modified so that it is both appropriate and fair. It must also recognize the differences among the disciplines and that faculty members have not only different strengths but, often, different roles, as well. And, most important, the faculty reward system must be sensitive to and supportive of what faculty members are required to do. Finally, there must be a clear understanding of what is meant by "scholarly work" and how it can be documented. The approach presented in this chapter is one attempt at providing this framework.

References

Boyer, E. *Scholarship Reconsidered: Priorities of the Professoriate.* Princeton, N.J.: The Carnegie Foundation for the Advancement of Teaching, 1990.

Diamond, R., and Adam, B. (eds.). *The Disciplines Speak: Rewarding the Scholarly, Professional, and Creative Work of Faculty.* Washington, D.C.: American Association for Higher Education, 1995.

Diamond, R., and Adam, B. (eds.). *The Disciplines Speak II: More Statements on Rewarding the Scholarly, Professional, and Creative Work of Faculty.* Washington, D.C.: American Association for Higher Education, 2000.

Diamond, R. M. "Changing Priorities and the Faculty Reward System." In Diamond, R. M., and Adam, B. E. *Recognizing Faculty Work: Reward Systems for the Year 2000.* New Directions in Higher Education, no. 81. San Francisco: Jossey-Bass, 1993.

Diamond, R. M. " *Aligning Faculty Rewards with Institutional Mission: Statements, Policies and Guidelines.* Bolton, Mass.: Anker, 1999.

Diamond, R. M., and Adam, B. E. *Changing Priorities at Research Universities: 1991–1996.* Syracuse, N.Y.: Center for Institutional Development, 1997.

Glassick, C. E., Huber, M. T., and Maeroff, G. I. *Scholarship Assessed: Evaluation of the Professoriate.* San Francisco: Jossey-Bass, 1997.

Rice, R. E. "The New American Scholar: Scholarship and the Purpose of the University." *Metropolitan Universities Journal,* 1991, *1*(4), 7–18.

Rice, R. E. *Making a Place for the New American Scholar.* Washington, D.C.: American Association of Higher Education, 1996.

Trower, C. A. (ed.). *Policies in Faculty Appointment.* Bolton, Mass.: Anker, 2000.

ROBERT M. DIAMOND is a research professor at Syracuse University, a visiting professor at the University of South Florida, St. Petersburg, and president of the National Academy of Academic Leadership. He is the author of numerous books and articles on tenure and promotions, as well as on course and curriculum design and assessment.

8

Collaborative inquiry-based education (undergraduate research, scholarship, and creative activity) and collaborative administrative models are this chapter's topics. Both mentoring undergraduate research projects and collaborative administrative action point to new ways of incorporating research and learning into a single integrated process.

Student-Faculty Collaborations, Undergraduate Research, and Collaboration as an Administrative Model

Ronald L. Dotterer

An ever-growing number of academics, including this author, see undergraduate research as the pedagogy for the twenty-first century. Inquiry-based learning, scholarship, and creative accomplishments have become commonplace at a majority of American doctoral and research institutions, comprehensive universities, and liberal arts colleges. This laudable success is attributable in part to the appealing nature of practicing undergraduate research, but, less obviously, it is also attributable to inclusive and comprehensive elements at the heart of undergraduate research itself. This new curricular approach combines teaching and research—two historic poles of a professional dichotomy, into one integrated pedagogy and system of performance—a new "vision" that scholarship and teaching may not be as separable as conventionally thought or practiced. In undergraduate research, teaching and scholarship, rather, become parts of one simultaneous, overlapping, shared process. This new pedagogy rejects the archetype of a scholar struggling alone with competing findings who is then forced to profess those or far-older discoveries to a group of as-yet uninformed students. Replacing this archetype is the collaborative investigative model, one using

For their guidance in how to collaborate and their willingness to do so, I am grateful to my fellow contemporary Salisbury deans: Beth Barnett (education and professional studies), Richard Bebee (business), and Tom Jones (science and technology).

research done with a mentoring model or done jointly by students and teachers—a new vision portending a major shift in how scholarship in the academy is practiced. Replacing competitive modes of inquiry with ones more focused on collective and collaborative work, this model of collaboration even offers an enlivening future alternative in academic leadership and institutional governance, as I try to lay out in the second half of this chapter. Either for student-faculty or for administrative-faculty interactions, collaboration offers an exciting and effective new heuristic.

Undergraduate research, therefore, is a comprehensive curricular innovation and major reform in contemporary American undergraduate education and scholarship. Its central premise is the formation of a collaborative enterprise between student and faculty member—most often one mentor and one burgeoning scholar, but sometimes (particularly in the social sciences) a team consisting of either one or both. This collaboration triggers the four-step learning process critical to the inquiry-based model and, congruently, several of its prime benefits: (1) identifying and acquiring a disciplinary or interdisciplinary methodology, (2) setting out a concrete investigative problem, (3) carrying out an actual project, and (4) sharing a new scholar's discoveries with his or her peers.

By incorporating both old and new strategies, undergraduate research motivates students to learn by doing. With faculty mentors, students engage directly in practicing the work of their discipline while they avoid passively acquiring knowledge that that discipline has produced. Not all of the elements of undergraduate research, of course, were recently born. For a long time, undergraduate students have carried out major research projects as part of their graduation requirements. Indeed, the research-based term paper is one of the fixtures of the undergraduate experience. Yet campuses that focus on undergraduate research have used this specific and explicit strategy to prepare students more effectively for academic careers and professional endeavors within the information age.

Undergraduate research programs promote both new research and a student's analytical and communicative skills from the student's first days within the college experience. As a by-product, these programs also create internal networks to support these efforts. Any campus that motivates its students to learn through individual and collaborative research—and can find ways to support these intellectual journeys with the necessary human and material resources—certainly does provide its students with a first-rate education.

The National Conferences on Undergraduate Research

The National Conferences on Undergraduate Research (NCUR®) is the largest professional organization devoted to fostering undergraduate research, scholarship, and creative accomplishments in all academic disciplines. Now in its fifteenth year, NCUR began as a project of the National

Science Foundation, the National Collegiate Honors Council, and a group of individuals at the University of North Carolina, Asheville, who yearned for a mechanism for undergraduates to measure their intellectual research efforts against peers from across the country. Funding from the Camille and Henry Dreyfus Foundation, the National Science Foundation, and the Petroleum Research Fund were critical to NCUR in its first decade. A second and equally important precept for NCUR, from its infancy, has been its conscious attempt to promote diversity among those who practice undergraduate research, seen most visibly in concrete efforts to increase the number of minority and underrepresented groups of students doing such research and making presentations of their work at NCUR or at national meetings of the professions.

Each year NCUR sponsors an annual conference where more than sixteen hundred undergraduates from over four hundred colleges and universities present their research in at least fifty-six academic disciplines. Four fields have historically represented more than half of those presentations: biology, chemistry, psychology, and physics. The phrase "research experience for undergraduates (REU)," now standard in the vocabulary of undergraduate research, came to us, too, from the National Science Foundation and from programs in the sciences. Yet the sciences and social sciences each year cede a bit more of their dominant ground in undergraduate research to other areas, including the fine arts and the humanities, so that the most recent conferences have had only a slim majority of presentations in the sciences.

Humanities departments have been the slowest to participate, despite the pioneering support of the National Endowment for the Humanities (NEH) for undergraduate research in its innovative Younger Scholars Program. An unwillingness to acknowledge the deep collaborative enterprise that was part of today's faculty members' own choices of Ph.D. dissertation sponsors, for example, often presents itself in more traditional humanities departments as resistance to the embracing of undergraduate research. The Younger Scholars Program, like too many functions of NEH, fell prey to the 1994 Congressional budget cuts and has not as yet been restored. Such a program, through its commitment to student inquiry, would do much to clarify the reasons for the importance of the humanities to the lives of a new generation. John Knecht and Robert McVaugh of Colgate University, Robert Dunning of the University of North Carolina, Asheville, and John Swift of Occidental College deserve mention for their leadership in the drive for increased participation of the fine arts and humanities in undergraduate research.

The Undergraduate Research Network is also part of each NCUR conference, with sessions focusing on the establishment and funding of programs, interdisciplinary approaches to undergraduate research, and the role of faculty mentors in the research process. This program, whose emphasis is on the mentor in the undergraduate research process, has done much to forge networks of practitioners in the specific disciplines and to share their experiences and discoveries of ways to stimulate student involvement in the research process.

A recent and exciting development of the organization is a joint project with the Alice and Leslie E. Lancy Foundation—the NCUR/Lancy grants to institutions for the advancement and spread of interdisciplinary undergraduate research programs at colleges and universities. To date, this project has brought $900,000 in grants to a variety of research, comprehensive, and liberal arts institutions of all sizes, in all regions of the United States.

Undergraduate Research at Salisbury University

Locally, at my current institution, Salisbury University, the promotion of undergraduate research, for example, has created a campuswide interdisciplinary discussion about how students learn and how research is conducted among and across the disciplines. In the arts and sciences and in the professional schools, students do theoretical and applied research, both as methods of learning along the way and as capstone experiences in their specific majors. Undergraduate research is a very effective assessment vehicle, for it requires the application of knowledge to actual situations on the part of each practitioner. Social work students, for example, have been particularly effective in investigating community-based issues such as housing and medical service delivery, as well as presenting analyses and solutions. Likewise, political science, environmental studies, and business majors have based their research on a local town's or municipality's actual community needs, directly benefiting the citizens of those communities and discovering key qualities of civic engagement themselves. Annual on-campus undergraduate research conferences recognize outstanding examples of undergraduate research and nurture a community of scholarly exchange among students and faculty members. Participation in NCUR or in one or more regional or national professional association meetings validates these student research efforts and creates a network for faculty members—both within a discipline and across disciplines all over the country—who are interested in promoting undergraduate research.

Coming to Collaboration as a Personal Model

How did I come to value collaborative work and this particular form of collaboration known as undergraduate research? I offer that history here (at the risk of narcissism but at the urging of this issue's editor), to demonstrate that, first, the practice of collaboration has played a key role in my own career. Mine is a commonplace academic journey that provides only anecdotal evidence. Its more important purpose is to demonstrate that we have been coming to an emphasis on undergraduate research for a long while and in true evolutionary style.

My acquaintance with undergraduate research, I confess, began long before I knew the term or formally subscribed to its pedagogical assumptions. As an undergraduate, for an honors thesis in English, I did a three-semester study of four twentieth-century poets: T. S. Eliot, Wallace Stevens, William Carlos Williams, and W. B. Yeats. The lengthy project that I wrote was an idiosyncratic look at the modern long poem as mythopoetic structure and alternate replacement for religion. I didn't know then that I was practicing undergraduate research; I was mostly working out personal business through this new vocabulary and methodology of literary criticism I'd so recently discovered.

As I look back on the weekly sessions I spent with my faculty mentor and compare them with the steps in this process that we now identify more explicitly, I recall my mentor's expectations for student practice, and there seems no other name for what I was doing than what it was—undergraduate research. I went off to graduate school and wrote a master's thesis and later a dissertation, comfortable with the central process of the enterprise (albeit not as comfortable with the actual labor!). Comprehending the methodology, and then designing and executing the project, I completed the process in my first graduate student presentations at the Northeast Modern Language Association, presenting my research to those I hoped would one day be my own peers.

The thirty years that follow have taken me to private and public institutions. Starting as a non-tenure-track English instructor, I landed a tenure-track line and made it through the tenure review and the traditional promotions—assistant, associate, and full. In 1981 I founded and directed an honors program, creating a four-year curriculum, designing a process of admission and evaluation for students in the program, and recruiting faculty members to teach within it. I spent a year as an American Council of Education Fellow and as an assistant to the president; then, an unplanned journey into administration led me to become a department chair, and then, most recently, I became dean (serving for eight years) of a liberal arts college within a comprehensive public university.

Surprisingly, for it has been by happenstance more than by honest intention, the act of collaboration has always been central to my life—as an administrator, as a collaborative teacher, as a collaborative scholarly writer, and as a day-to-day collaborator with my decanal colleagues within an institution. I first began to think about collaboration in the late 1970s, when I joined something called the Collaboration for Undergraduate Education network (CUE), founded by William Whipple, formerly of the University of Maine and Albright College, Sara Varhus, dean of arts and sciences at Oswego State University, and Karin Roemer, associate dean of arts and sciences at Brown University. Contemporaneously, as part of three NEH-funded grant projects, I team-taught courses for the first time. Several of those courses used film as a vehicle for exploring the humanities. A philosophy professor and I taught the courses as a team and wrote an article together, seeking language that was interdisciplinary in describing film study. Another course involved a dozen faculty members designing and teaching together a common literary course for all undergraduates. My involvement with honors education made me a convert to the cause of faculty members and students working directly together, for an effective honors program needs the efficient efforts of almost all parts of a college or university as it models ways for faculty members and students to work and learn together.

Getting involved with NCUR brought the final slam of the door behind me. I'm now a full-scale convert. I can see that my work in the national initiative to advance undergraduate research has benefited the institutions of which I've been a part, but—more selfishly—it has also brought me significant satisfaction in my own interdisciplinary professional life, as well as some of my highest moments of professional satisfaction in general.

The Efficacy of Undergraduate Research

Ten of the twelve quality attributes of outstanding undergraduate education, identified by the Education Commission for the States (1995) as their description of what is fundamental in quality undergraduate education, apply directly to this new blossoming of undergraduate education. They are: (1) high expectations, (2) respect for diverse talents and learning styles, (3) the synthesizing of experiences, (4) the ongoing practice of learned skills, (5) the integration of education and experience, (6) active learning, (7) assessment and prompt feedback, (8) collaboration, (9) adequate time on task, and (10) out-of-class contact with faculty members. The remaining two attributes—emphasis on early years of study and coherence in learning—while not necessary to an undergraduate research model of instruction, are certainly supportive of this pedagogy and its attendant outcomes and are likely to be growing components as inquiry-based education plays an increasing role in first courses in the major and in the design of core curricula.

A March 2001 summit meeting at the University of Kentucky of ten professional organizations interested in undergraduate research had as one of its central conclusions the need for a corpus of concrete research in a variety of disciplines that demonstrates clearly what is still largely laudatory or anecdotal evidence that undergraduate research is a superior methodology for undergraduate instruction. Hosted by NCUR, the other nine organizations represented were the Alice and Leslie E. Lancy Foundation, the American Association of Colleges and Universities, the American Association for Higher Education, the Council on Undergraduate Research, the National Collegiate Honors Council, the National Science Foundation, Phi Beta Kappa, Project Kaleidoscope, and Sigma Xi. The Carnegie Commission on Teaching's report (1998), which asks research universities to integrate their missions of research and teaching, is another backdrop for work that demonstrates the value of this integration.

Administrative Collaboration

Just as teaching has traditionally been seen as a solitary activity, administrative structures of colleges and universities have emphasized clear hierarchical models of leadership that mirror those in place in corporate, political, and ecclesiastical worlds. Shared presidencies not only are rare but are also largely outside conservative academic imaginations. Nicholas Murray Butler, William Friday, and Father Theodore Hesburgh are three very different male models from the past century, demonstrating that strong and enduring academic leadership has depended upon clear and consistent direction from a single figure, no matter how enlightened a collaborator that person may have been. Yet, each year, more women, minorities, and less traditionally trained white males lead these very traditional institutions. Hence, each year this traditional notion of leadership expands a bit further to encompass more complex and even subversive notions of joint activities and provides new alternatives to more time-honored structures for direction setting and strategic leadership.

Every person in charge knows that the competitive method of resource allocation can result—whether in government or in education—in a fairly permanent division among the haves and have-nots. Sometimes, forming a team is the more effective means to proceed. During a period of appreciable senior administrative turnover, with relative stability among the academic deans, my fellow deans and I (again, by happenstance as much as by deliberate action) found that sometimes a collaborative model worked more effectively than a corporate or competitive model in doing the actual academic work of the university. Whether the issue was allocating dollars for equipment or for merit pay, or designing the case statements for a new capital campaign, the needs of the schools and colleges were more effectively met when their respective leaders could work together with the leaders of the other units. We decided these issues together by debate and negotiation, leading to consensus. Despite our various disciplinary pasts, as deans, we set out the common investigative problem, carried our work through to an actual solution, and finally, as part of the dispersal of that discovery, made a collective presentation of our results.

In addition, three of these local deans have for the past few years led seminars around the country on implementing collaborative roles between education and arts-and-sciences schools and colleges in reforming teacher education. All of the four deans tried to follow this collaborative model in deans' forums, urging faculty members who are often more competitive with one another than collaborative to work across these historic divides. I thank Wyatt Anderson, dean of arts and sciences at the University of Georgia, for demonstrating the merits of the deans' forum as a means of modeling behavior and for simultaneously bringing together faculty members who would otherwise communicate infrequently.

One tale I told often to the school's department chairs is that, as a school, we sometimes acted as if we were the city-states of Renaissance Italy.

We could and did hire a "pope" to make marriages and annul them, but this secular pontiff had better stay within the walls of the Vatican rather than cross the borders of any one of the neighboring "city-states." An alliance between the pope and one's enemy state seems particularly threatening and problematic, for academic departments and schools within a university still have the same distrust of competing units that Renaissance Italy demonstrated in its political life. The famous metaphor used too frequently in describing the governance structure of colleges and universities is one of *silos*, whose operations are distinct and independent on the farm. But collaboration among departments is possible. This past spring, for example, ten heads of those city-states agreed unanimously on a priority order for new faculty positions. Even issues that bring out self-interest can, in the best climate of debate and negotiation, find their common enterprise with enough investigation.

Effective work, as all mentors and those who have worked successfully with mentors know, comes when trust is at the center of individual action. If colleges and universities could ensure that trust was present among its parts, levels of attainment would rapidly increase. Whether in the traditional hierarchy of teacher/scholar above student or of academic leader above the person reporting to that leader, collaboration is the central dimension of the new heuristic of using research as a model for guiding teaching and administration. Undergraduate research has already taught us (and collaborative administrative action will, I hope, one day guide us toward) the goal of the mentoring process: to achieve a fully integrated and effective model for learning.

References

Dunning, R. "Undergraduate Research in the Fine Arts: The UNC-Asheville Curriculum." *Council on Undergraduate Research Quarterly,* March 1994, pp. 136–37.

Hakim, T. M. *At the Interface of Scholarship and Teaching: How to Develop and Administer Institutional Undergraduate Research Programs.* Washington, D.C: Council on Undergraduate Research, 2000.

Kenny, S. S., and Associates. *Reinventing Undergraduate Education: A Blueprint for America's Research Universities.* The Boyer Commission on Educating Undergraduates in the Research University. Stony Brook, NY: Carnegie Foundation for the Advancement of Teaching, 1998. [http://naples.cc.sunysb.edu/Pres/boyer.nsf]

Nagda, B. A., and others. "Undergraduate Student-Faculty Research Partnerships Affect Student Retention." *Review of Higher Education,* 1998, 22(1), 55–72.

Romer, R., Ewell, P., Jones, D., and Lenth, C. *Making Quality Count in Undergraduate Education.* Denver: Education Commission for the States, 1995. This report is available for $13 from ECS Distribution Center, 707 17th St., Suite 2700, Denver, Colo. 80202. A synopsis appeared in *AAHE Bulletin,* Apr. 1996, pp. 5–8.

Schowen, K. B. *Research as a Critical Component of the Undergraduate Educational Experience.* Washington, D.C., National Academy Press, 1998.

Strassburger, J. "Embracing Undergraduate Research." *AAHE Bulletin,* May 1995, pp. 3–5.

Volkwein, J. F., and Carbone, D. "The Impact of Departmental Research and Teaching Climates on Undergraduate Growth and Satisfaction." *Journal of Higher Education,* 1994, 65(2), 146–67.

Werner, T. C., Lichter, R. L., and Krugh, T. R. "The National Conference on Undergraduate Research (NCUR): Conference History and the Role of Chemistry." *Journal of Chemical Education,* May 2001, 78(5), 691–694.

Resources

For information on the National Conferences on Undergraduate Research (NCUR), its annual conference, the Lancy/NCUR research grants, and its home base at Union College, visit its Web site at http://www.ncur.org. For information on the Council on Undergraduate Research, a complementary organization emphasizing faculty development in the sciences and, more recently, the social sciences, in undergraduate institutions, visit their Web site at http://www.cur.org. For information on Project Kaleidoscope, an initiative whose chief aim is the reform of science education, visit its Web site at http://www.pkal.org.

RONALD L. DOTTERER, *professor of English and dean (1993–2001) at the Charles R. and Martha N. Fulton School of Liberal Arts, Salisbury University, is currently chair of the National Conferences on Undergraduate Research (NCUR), and his books include those on Shakespeare; Irish literature; Jewish settlement and community in the modern world; and women, the arts, and society.*

*Rising expectations of higher education, the lackluster
performance of K–12 education, declining participation
in American civic life, and concerns about a deteriorating
community infrastructure and difficult social issues
provide new scholarly opportunities through community
engagement. The postmodern era requires developing new
epistemologies if this scholarship of community
engagement is to flower and mature.*

Nurturing an Ethos of Community Engagement

Jerry Berberet

Community engagement in higher education is, of course, not new. It is part of the historic service mission of colleges and universities. Community service, or "outreach," is included routinely in institutional mission statements and is listed as a faculty responsibility in virtually every faculty handbook. Yet, with the possible exception of the land-grant university, service has remained poorly defined, largely disconnected from research and teaching, and rarely conceived in terms of scholarship. Thus, aside from its Deweyan philosophical origins, the emergence of a *scholarship* of community engagement awaited Ernest Boyer's broadening of the definition of scholarship (1990) and a convergence of influences over the past decade that have forged a new self-consciousness about the purposes of higher education, the nature of learning, and the epistemological relationships between the scholar and the context of scholarly inquiry.

Setting the Stage for a Scholarship of Community Engagement

Ernest Boyer (1994) called for a "New American College" that would take "special pride in its capacity to connect thought to action, theory to practice" (p. A48) on behalf of America's communities. In doing so, Boyer believed that such institutions would renew the tradition of service to society that he associated with nineteenth-century liberal arts and land-grant colleges, which he believed higher education had abandoned in the twentieth century. Echoing Boyer, Russell Edgerton (1997) declared that American higher education had become self-preoccupied, losing its historic sense of a mission of social significance, and he urged faculty members to step forward to reclaim a legacy. Alexander Astin (1991) has countered higher education's fascination with institutional prestige based on student selectivity and amassing resources by arguing that excellence ought rather to be based on the quality of outcomes a college or university produces—a value-added measure. Why not outcomes through community engagement?

Meanwhile, the focus was shifting on campus from faculty teaching to student learning (Barr, 1995), with emphasis on active learning—problem-based learning, service learning, and learning communities—and assessment of learning outcomes. Students demanded that learning have greater practical and social consequence, as witnessed by the career concerns of an increasingly diverse student population and the growing popularity of service learning programs. Moreover, cognitive research substantiates that applied learning and problem solving, engaging what Carol Geary Schneider (2001) has labeled "unscripted problems," produce understanding and competency superior to acquiring theoretical knowledge alone (National Research Council, 1999). By the late 1990s, faculty-student research had blossomed on campuses across the country, including research on issues and problems in the regional community within reach of the campus. And, more and more, institutions are getting into the act, developing school and community partnerships and encouraging among faculty members what Burton Clark (2002) has called a spirit of "collegial entrepreneurialism."

The idea of moving from modernism to a postmodern era, although simplistic, involves a paradigm shift for which a scholarship of community engagement is a logical expression. Modernism has been associated with a platonic focus on timeless verities, adherence to a relatively unchanging canon, and epistemologies anchored in theoretical abstractions, tested at best under controlled conditions in a laboratory. The modernist worldview disdains involvement in the world because such contact invites a subjectivity that places "value-free" inquiry at risk. Modernism accentuated a dualism separating knowledge and experience, theory and practice, and mind and soul from body that some have traced to Bacon and Descartes, and some to Augustine of Hippo (Craige, 1988). In American higher education during the twentieth century, modernism represented a triumph of detached objectivity over both a Deweyan epistemology that looked ultimately to community experience for validation and the 1960s scholarship of protest and relativity. Modernism also turned away from Whitehead's admonitions against "inert" ideas that had not passed a worldly test of utility and his advocacy of a "seamless coat of learning" linking general and specialized knowledge and knowledge and experience (1929).

Yet modernism has never enjoyed an unchallenged reign. The intellectual forces conspiring against it include the "isms" of a changing society—for example, multiculturalism, feminism, and environmentalism—and the deconstructionist critique within the academy, especially the humanities, that ignited the tumultuous culture wars beginning in the 1970s. Indeed,

Allen Bloom's ink in *The Closing of the American Mind* (1987) was barely dry before Boyer (1990) articulated his compelling scholarship of integration, challenging the modernist focus on the scholarship of discovery to embrace, as well, scholarships of application, interdisciplinary work, and, ultimately, the practice of teaching. Modernism was also wounded by the public criticism—in many ways unfair—that a self-centered, disengaged academy was responsible for educational ills ranging from poorly educated graduates to the wrong-headed allocation of resources, ills epitomized for many in a faculty with light teaching loads and practicing scholarship of dubious utilitarian value—to which Boyer's scholarships offered a positive response.

Scholarship Reconsidered has stimulated a rethinking of scholarship and faculty roles across higher education. This "unbundling" of faculty work, for example, prompted Oregon State University to redefine scholarship to fit the context of a faculty member's primary responsibilities, whether laboratory research or extension outreach, and to make each faculty member responsible for scholarly activity related to these responsibilities (Weiser, 1998). Such "contextualizing" of scholarship is also taking place at Arizona State University, where President Lattie Coor (2000) has taken the report of the Kellogg Commission on the Future of State and Land Grant Universities to heart in pursuing an institutional strategy of community engagement as an acid test for demonstrating the University's future relevance. Responding to concerns about declining citizen participation in the nation's civic life and eager to have their institutions demonstrate a commitment to community engagement, more than two hundred presidents signed Campus Compact's 1999 Presidents' Fourth of July Declaration on the Civic Responsibility of Higher Education. In part, the Declaration reads, "We also challenge higher education to become engaged, through actions and teaching with its communities."

Eugene Rice (1996) proposes a faculty professional model, which he characterizes as the "Complete Scholar," in which he conceives faculty roles as a complementary whole and relates them to institutional and community well-being. Rice argues that the faculty career should be viewed as a continuum in which needs and interests may change over time. The constant is a process of scholarly maturation reflective of an increasingly sophisticated integration of research, teaching, and campus and community service. In a follow-up work to *Scholarship Reconsidered* that was published after Boyer's death, the Carnegie Foundation for the Advancement of Teaching advocated that all faculty work, including work typically categorized as service, be susceptible to evaluation by common scholarly standards, in effect creating a platform for legitimating a scholarship of community engagement (Glassick, Huber, and Maeroff, 1997). The Associated New American Colleges (ANAC), a national consortium of twenty private comprehensive institutions, has taken the additional step of calling for a self-conscious alignment of faculty work policies, practices, and rewards with an institutional mission. ANAC contends that such a "compact" would serve as a cornerstone for a faculty-institutional mutuality that would nourish a flowering of Rice's Complete Scholar (McMillin, 2001).

The postmodern sense of an interdependent and integrated whole—with connections between campus and community, mutuality between faculty and institution, a coherent faculty professional model, and the notion of a symbiotic relationship between thought and action and knowledge and experience, which Boyer and Dewey shared—has created an environment in which the scholarship of community engagement can flourish. In particular, there is growing recognition that the educational enterprise derives its vitality from the excitement engagement in learning generates, which is critical to the purposeful functioning of institutions and the scholarly focus of the faculty, as well as being necessary for student learning. Peter Senge (1990) has described the generative capacity of the "learning organization." Jon Wergin (2001) reminds us that meaningful intellectual engagement is the primary motivator for faculty members, followed closely by a yearning to be a member of a community in which one can have an impact and gain recognition. In reflecting on faculty vitality in the postmodern era, the scholarship of community engagement plays a primary role in satisfying these needs.

An Epistemology for the Scholarship of Community Engagement

Constructing an epistemology for the scholarship of community engagement requires both the rethinking of the nature and purposes of scholarship that Boyer initiated and assumptions about truth and ground rules for determining it that are consistent with the emerging paradigms of the postmodern era. For starters, attempts by scholars to present the findings of their empirical research as the whole "truth" in engaging the larger community are being met with increasing skepticism within and without the academy. Not only is theoretical research that is untested in the court of community experience suspect, but postmodernism implies that both the nature of the research and the research methodologies employed must result from participation of the interest groups and the general population (the "stakeholders"), who may be affected by the results of the research (London, 1999). These ground rules extend beyond the civil rights principle at work in the protection of human subjects in social science or medical research. And such inclusion and participation is also emerging as a sine qua non of a postmodern scholarship of community engagement for ethical and epistemological reasons.

Donald Schon (1987) made monumental contributions to the development of a postmodern scholarly epistemology. In seminal works of the 1980s, he borrowed from the studio tradition in the arts and professions to describe a process he called "reflection in action"—reflection on the interaction of theory and practice—as the core intellectual activity that should run through faculty research, teaching, and learning. Because professional practice is essential to what studio faculty members do—whether it's music, architecture, or engineering—Schon coined the term "reflective practitioner" in calling for faculty engagement in the consequences of their work. Shortly before his death, a decade later, Schon argued that institutions and faculty members alike must adopt a new epistemology in order to practice Boyer's multiple scholarships. He contended that "action research"—his term for a scholarship of community engagement—requires not only that institutions and faculty members move beyond the epistemology of technical rationality the German research university conferred on the scholarship of discovery but that they also engage in "reflective action research." According to Schon (1995), reflective action research obligates scholars to reflect on both their scholarly knowing and their scholarly methodologies in an ongoing way.

Schon's work provides a partial blueprint for a scholarship of community engagement, but it does not fully prepare the scholar to transcend the scholar-centered rationality of studio or laboratory in order to engage the community with assumptions, questions, hypotheses, and methodologies open to community input. In other words, a full-blown scholarship of community engagement requires the university and the scholar to undertake a scholarly endeavor in which control is shared with community participants.

Fortunately, others have addressed what Schon did not. In its efforts to develop an epistemology of public scholarship, the Kettering Foundation has noted that the community participants' ways of knowing have scholarly authenticity independent of public scholar "reinterpretation" (Boyte, 2000). As have feminist humanities scholars, public scholars are learning to give voice to community members through such devices as narrative, which captures the language, interpretations, and anecdotes—in other words, the truth-telling of the community—and presents them in unvarnished form. Inspired by efforts to foster inclusion, to educate students for responsible citizenship, and to engage communities, scholars of the democratic process are rediscovering insights of which the founders had some inkling—that listening, democratic dialogue, and open decision making level the playing field and inspire the participation necessary for a scholarship of community engagement to evolve that has credibility in a postmodern world (Guarasci, 1997; Schneider, 2001).

Finally, a scholarship of community engagement requires holistic perspectives and role-modeling responsibilities that pose daunting challenges to institutions and scholars. It seems inescapable, however, that unless campuses and scholars practice the educational and scholarly values they preach, the academy will achieve at best a limited moral authority, and higher education will struggle to regain the significance accorded it when a college education was seen more widely as a public good. David Orr (1992) writes of the necessity for campuses to become models of sustainable communities, especially by taking responsibility for their consumption of energy and resources and the recycling of the waste they produce, as a prerequisite for a fully credible scholarship of environmental management and protection. Noel Perrin's recent scorecard on how well colleges and universities are doing in becoming environmentally friendly (2001) suggests that the academy still has a long way to go in passing this test of a scholarship of community engagement in the postmodern era.

The New American College: An Institutional Model for the Scholarship of Community Engagement

Boyer's call for a "New American College" (1994) encouraged higher education to ponder the characteristics of what would be a uniquely American synthesis, both as a form of scholarship and as an institutional model for higher education. He noted that the American colonial liberal arts college found its seventeenth- and eighteenth-century roots at Oxford and Cambridge and that the nineteenth-century research university had German origins. The land-grant college had a uniquely American extension service mission in developing communities that Boyer sought to revive in calling for a "sturdy American hybrid" that would combine the best features of these institutional antecedents in renewing a tradition of higher education service to community.

After a several-year dialogue with Boyer, a national group of primarily Carnegie classification Masters I and II comprehensive institutions founded the Associated New American Colleges in 1995. Seeking to better understand their identity in a land where everyone understands the nature of liberal arts colleges and research universities, the ANAC members recognized that they possessed the distinctive features of all three institutional antecedents: (1) like liberal arts colleges, they emphasized core liberal arts education for traditional-age students in small residential campus communities where classes are small and faculty members have a primary commitment to educating "one student at a time," (2) like research universities, they had a diverse residential and commuter student body of all ages and a variety of liberal arts, professional, and graduate programs, and (3) like the land-grant research universities, they had a strong identification with the communities in which they were located, both in seeing their own growth and development parallel community demographic and economic patterns, and in their commitment to serve the educational, cultural, and economic needs of their communities.

ANAC members then determined that their strategic opportunity lay in combining these shared qualities synergistically in order to make a virtue of their hybrid character and, mindful of their modest resources, to develop their institutional capacities. They recognized that being manageably sized (having fewer than ten thousand students) enabled them to act with a unity of purpose impossible at a large research university. By the same token, their diversity of programs proved to be a virtue because it provided them with professional faculty expertise in areas ranging from business, law, engineering, and architecture to the allied health sciences that simply are not present at liberal arts colleges.

Consequently, and in keeping with familiar institutional traditions, many ANAC members have engaged their communities in ambitious development and renewal partnerships, ranging from school reform and shared cultural facilities to inner-city housing and social services, and from ambitious economic development projects to planning for environmental protection. Reflecting a hybrid strategy, these undertakings routinely connect learning and scholarship, faculty members and students, liberal and professional studies, and campus and community participants. The similarity of these connections with the educational ideas of John Dewey and the postmodernist philosopher Richard Rorty led one observer to offer the New American College as an emerging postmodern institutional model of higher education (DeNicola, 1994).

The example of Mercer University and its Mercer Community Development Center is a case in point. Working with local government, school districts, and inner-city neighborhood residents adjacent to campus, liberal arts and professional program faculty members and students have undertaken interdisciplinary housing, social services, school improvement, and economic development research and service projects. Funding has been attracted from a variety of foundation and federal sources, including the John S. and James L. Knight Foundation, the Lilly Endowment, and the federal departments of Education and Housing and Urban Development, to underwrite a variety of projects. Moreover, the Lilly grant is supporting a campuswide rethinking of the "calling," or "vocation," that animates the University's educational and service missions, an impetus for purposeful integration of Mercer's campus and community goals, which is consistent with postmodern thinking.

Several other examples illustrate the range of ANAC member scholarship of community engagement. The University of Hartford's new elementary magnet school, on the theme of Howard Gardner's multiple intelligences, enrolls students from six nearby inner-city and suburban schools and serves as a multidisciplinary research setting for University faculty members and students. The University of Redlands coordinates a $4 million federally funded research project involving the threatened environment of the nearby Salton Sea. Elon University has attracted national recognition for its faculty-student research program—affiliated with the Carnegie Academy for the Scholarship of Teaching and Learning, which links faculty engagement across the disciplines with Elon's focus on experiential learning and community service.

Community engagement on the part of ANAC members is notable not because it is occurring but because it happens easily and organically as a natural extension of the dominant mode of campus teaching, learning, and scholarship. But community engagement is happening nationwide at all types of institutions—so much so that the term "engaged campus" is becoming commonplace (Gamson, Hollander, and Kiang, 1998; Thomas, 1999). At Oregon's Portland State University, the mission is focused on community engagement: "Let knowledge serve the city." At the University of Illinois, the East St. Louis Action Research Project engages faculty members and students from arts and sciences and professional programs with elected and school officials and neighborhood activists across ethnic, religious, and class boundaries to generate jobs, affordable housing, and school reform (Reardon, 1999). At Wagner College, students engage in community-based research on the arts of democracy in community problem solving as part of a service-learning curricular requirement. National higher education associations have also gotten into the act. For example, the Association of American Colleges and Universities' Project SENCER (Science Education for New Civic Engagements and Responsibilities), funded by the National Science Foundation, engages students at AACU member institutions in multidisciplinary investigations of the scientific, social, policy, and ethical issues that surround HIV. SENCER fosters civic education, produces new knowledge, and places that knowledge in the service of larger moral aims (Burns, 2001).

Summary and Prospects

Much like the academy's engagement in postmodernism itself, the scholarship of community engagement occurs by degrees, ranging from community-based research around economic development and public policy issues to full-fledged and highly self-conscious mission-driven engagement with communities. The latter is truly collaborative in its relationship with community partners, is interdisciplinary in focus, and is connected intrinsically to faculty and student scholarship and learning. It is generative, capable of transforming colleges and universities in their ability to meet rising educational expectations—whether workforce-related to supply a sophisticated information economy, civic-related to renew a democracy many fear is at risk, or development-related to rebuild an aging community infrastructure.

Nurturing a scholarship of community engagement begins with the assumption that establishing a democratic campus-community relationship is a precondition for creating an authentic context for community-based research and analysis. The New American College institutional model is instructive because its ethos is one of connections and shared self-interest that promotes institutional integration and community partnership conducive to long-term sustainabiliy of both campus and community. In the postmodern sense, ANAC members see their local regions as contexts in which the institution and the community have the opportunity to construct together a shared future that each will either find beneficial or from which each will suffer adverse consequences. The urgent needs of our communities and the missions and latent capacities of our colleges and universities are such that one would have to look long and hard to find a more important purpose with greater potential for higher education than the scholarship of community engagement.

References

Astin, A. W. *Assessment for Excellence: The Philosophy and Practice of Assessment and Evaluation in Higher Education.* Old Tappan, N.J.: MacMillan, 1991.

Barr, R. B., and Tagg, J. "From Teaching to Learning: A New Paradigm for Undergraduate Education." *Change,* 1995, 27(6), 12–25.

Bloom, A. *The Closing of the American Mind.* New York: Simon & Schuster, 1987.

Boyer, E. L. *Scholarship Reconsidered: Priorities of the Professoriate.* Princeton, N.J.: The Carnegie Foundation for the Advancement of Teaching, 1990.

Boyer, E. L. "Creating the New American College." *Chronicle of Higher Education,* March 9, 1994, p. A48.

Boyer, E. L. "The New American College." *Perspectives,* 1994, 24(1–2), 6–12.

Boyte, H. "Public Work: An Interview with Harry Boyte." *Higher Education Exchange,* 2000. The Kettering Foundation, pp. 43–51.

Burns, D. "The Engaged Academy." *Liberal Education,* 2001, 87(1), 2–3.

Clark, B. R. "Collegial Entrepreneurialism in Proactive Universities: Lessons from Europe." *Change,* 2000, 32(5), 10–19.

Coor, L. F. "Universities of the Future Will Focus on Community Engagement." Paper presented at the National Association of College and University Business Officers Conference, Chicago, July 24, 2000.

Craige, B. J. *Reconnection: Dualism to Holism in Literary Study.* Athens: University of Georgia Press, 1988.

DeNicola, D. R. "The Emergence of the New American College." *Perspectives,* 1994, 24(1–2), 63–78.

Edgerton, R. *Higher Education White Paper.* Report of The Pew Charitable Trusts, Philadelphia, 1997.

Gamson, Z., Hollander, E., and Kiang, P. N. "The University in Engagement with Society." *Liberal Education,* 1998, 84(2), 20–25.

Glassick, C. E., Huber, M. T., and Maeroff, G. I. *Scholarship Assessed: Evaluation of the Professoriate.* Princeton: The Carnegie Foundation for the Advancement of Teaching, 1997.

Guarasci, R. *Democratic Education in an Age of Difference.* San Francisco: Jossey-Bass, 1997.

London, S. "The Academy and Public Life: Healing the Rift." *Higher Education Exchange,* 1999. The Kettering Foundation, pp. 4–15.

McMillin, L. A., and Berberet, J. (eds.). *A New Academic Compact: Revisioning the Relationship between Faculty and Their Institutions.* Bolton, Mass.: Anker, 2001.

National Research Council. *How People Learn: Brain, Mind, Experience, and School.* Washington, D.C.: National Academy Press, 1999.

Orr, D. W. *Ecological Literacy: Education and the Transition to a Postmodern World.* Albany: State University of New York Press, 1992.

Perrin, N. "The Greenest Campuses: An Idiosyncratic Guide." *Chronicle of Higher Education,* Apr. 6, 2001, pp. B7–10.

Reardon, K. "A Sustainable Community/University Partnership." *Liberal Education,* 1999, 85(3), 20–25.

Rice, R. E. "Making a Place for the New American Scholar." *Working Paper #1,* New Pathways Project, American Association for Higher Education, 1996.

Schneider, C. G. "Toward an Engaged Academy: New Scholarship, New Teaching." *Liberal Education,* 2001, 87(1), 18–27.

Schon, D. A. *Educating the Reflective Practitioner: Toward a New Design for Teaching and Learning in the Professions.* San Francisco: Jossey-Bass, 1987.

Schon, D. A. "The New Scholarship Requires a New Epistemology: Knowing in Action." *Change,* 1995, 16(6), 26–34.

Senge, P. M. *The Fifth Discipline: The Art and Practice of the Learning Organization.* New York: Doubleday Currency, 1990.

Thomas, N. L., and Hirsch, D. "Practicing and Modeling the 'Arts of Democracy': Higher Education's Renewed Civic Commitment." *Higher Education Exchange,* 1999. The Kettering Foundation, pp. 58–73.

Weiser, C. J., and Houglum, L. "Scholarship Unbound for the 21st Century." *Journal of Extension,* 1998, 36(4). [http://www.joe.org]

Wergin, J. F. "Beyond Carrots and Sticks: What Really Motivates Faculty." *Liberal Education,* 2001, 87(1), 50–53.

Whitehead, A. N. *Aims of Education.* Old Tappan, N.J.: Macmillan, 1929.

JERRY BERBERET *is an American historian and former academic administrator and is now executive director of the Associated New American Colleges.*

INDEX

Back Issue/Subscription Order Form

Copy or detach and send to:

Jossey-Bass, A Wiley Company, 989 Market Street, San Francisco CA 94103-1741

Call or fax toll-free: Phone 888-378-2537 6AM-5PM PST; Fax 888-481-2665

Back issues: Please send me the following issues at $27 each

(Important: please include series initials and issue number, such as TL85)

1. TL _____

_____

_____

$ _____Total for single issues

$ _____ SHIPPING CHARGES: SURFACE

	Domestic	Canadian
First Item	$5.00	$6.50
Each Add'l Item	$3.00	$3.00

For next-day and second-day delivery rates, call the number listed above.

Subscriptions   Please ❑ start ❑ renew my subscription to *New Directions for Teaching and Learning* for the year 2____ at the following rate:

U.S.	❑ Individual $65	❑ Institutional $130
Canada	❑ Individual $65	❑ Institutional $170
All Others	❑ Individual $89	❑ Institutional $204

$ _____Total single issues and subscriptions (Add appropriate sales tax for your state for single issue orders. No sales tax for U.S. subscriptions. Canadian residents, add GST for subscriptions and single issues.)

Federal Tax ID 135593032   GST 89102 8052

❑ Payment enclosed (U.S. check or money order only)

❑ VISA, MC, AmEx, Discover Card # _____ Exp. date_____

Signature _____ Day phone _____

❑ Bill me (U.S. institutional orders only. Purchase order required)

Purchase order #_____

Name _____

Address _____

_____

Phone_____ E-mail _____

For more information about Jossey-Bass, visit our Web site at: www.josseybass.com

PROMOTION CODE = ND3

Save Now on the Best of ABOUT CAMPUS Series Sets Enriching the Student Learning Experience

Dedicated to the idea that student learning is the responsibility of all educators on campus, **About Campus** illuminates critical issues faced by both student affairs and academic affairs staff as they work on the shared goal that brought them to the same campus in the first place: to help students learn.

With each issue, **About Campus** combines the imagination and creativity found in the best magazines and the authority and thoughtfulness found in the best professional journals. Now we've taken the four most popular issues from three volume years and we've made them available as a set—at a tremendous savings over our $20.00 single-issue price.

Best of About Campus – Volume 3
Facts and Myths About Assessment in Student Affairs – Why Learning Communities? Why Now? – The Stressed Student: How Can We Help? – Being All That We Can Be
ISBN 0–7879–6128–0 $12.00

Best of About Campus – Volume 4
Increasing Expectations for Student Effort – The Matthew Shepard Tragedy: Crisis and Beyond – Civic and Moral Learning – Faculty-Student Affairs Collaboration on Assessment.
ISBN 0–7879–6129–9 $12.00

Best of About Campus – Volume 5
The Diversity Within – What Can We Do About Student Cheating? – Bonfire: Tragedy and Tradition – Hogwarts: The Learning Community.
ISBN 0–7879–6130–2 $12.00

To order by phone: call 1–800–956–7739 or 415–433–1740

Visit our website at www.josseybass.com

Use promotion code **ND2** to guarantee your savings.
Shipping and applicable taxes will be added.

ABOUT CAMPUS

Sponsored by the *American College Personnel Association*
Published by Jossey-Bass, A Wiley Company
Patricia M. King, Executive Editor
Jon C. Dalton, Senior Editor

Published bimonthly. Individual subscriptions $53.00. Institutional subscriptions $95.00.

Jossey-Bass, A Wiley Company • 989 Market St., Fifth Floor • San Francisco, CA 94103–1741

TL84 Principles of Effective Teaching in the Online Classroom
Renée E. Weiss, Dave S. Knowlton, Bruce W. Speck
Discusses structuring the online course, utilizing resources from the World
Wide Web and using other electronic tools and technology to enhance
classroom efficiency. Addresses challenges unique to the online classroom
community, including successful communication strategies, performance
evaluation, academic integrity, and accessibility for disabled students.
ISBN: 0-7879-5615-5

TL83 Evaluating Teaching in Higher Education: A Vision for the Future
Katherine E. Ryan
Analyzes the strengths and weaknesses of current approaches to evaluating
teaching and recommends practical strategies for improving current
evaluation methods and developing new ones. Provides an overview of new
techniques such as peer evaluations, portfolios, and student ratings of
instructors and technologies.
ISBN: 0-7879-5448-9

TL82 Teaching to Promote Intellectual and Personal Maturity: Incorporating
Students' Worldviews and Identities into the Learning Process
Marcia B. Baxter Magolda
Explores cognitive and emotional dimensions that influence how individuals
learn, and describes teaching practices for building on these to help students
develop intellectually and personally. Examines how students' unique
understanding of their individual experience, themselves, and the ways
knowledge is constructed can mediate learning.
ISBN: 0-7879-5446-2

TL81 Strategies for Energizing Large Classes: From Small Groups to Learning
Communities
Jean MacGregor, James L. Cooper, Karl A. Smith, Pamela Robinson
Describes a comprehensive range of ideas and techniques from informal
turn-to-your-neighbor discussions that punctuate a lecture to more complex
small-group activities, as well as ambitious curricular reform through
learning-community structures.
ISBN: 0-7879-5337-7

TL80 Teaching and Learning on the Edge of the Millennium: Building on What
We Have Learned
Marilla D. Svinicki
Reviews the past and current research on teaching, learning, and motivation.
Chapters revisit the best-selling *NDTL* issues, exploring the latest
developments in group-based learning, effective communication, teaching
for critical thinking, the seven principles for good practice in undergraduate
education, teaching for diversity, and teaching in the information age.
ISBN: 0-7879-4874-8

TL79 Using Consultants to Improve Teaching
Christopher Knapper, Sergio Piccinin
Provides advice on how to use consultation to improve teaching, giving
detailed descriptions of a variety of effective approaches, including
classroom observation, student focus groups, small-group instructional
diagnosis, faculty learning communities, and action learning.
ISBN: 0-7879-4876-4

TL78   Motivation from Within: Approaches for Encouraging Faculty and
        Students to Excel
        Michael Theall
        Examines how students' cultural backgrounds and beliefs about knowledge
        affect their motivation to learn, and applies the latest motivational theory to
        the instructional process and the university community.
        ISBN: 0-7879-4875-6

TL77   Promoting Civility: A Teaching Challenge
        Steven M. Richardson
        Offers strategies for promoting civil discourse and resolving conflict when it
        arises—both in the classroom and in the campus community at large.
        Recommends effective responses to disruptive classroom behavior and
        techniques for encouraging open, respectful discussion of sensitive topics.
        ISBN: 0-7879-4277-4

TL76   The Impact of Technology on Faculty Development, Life, and Work
        Kay Herr Gillespie
        Describes ways to enhance faculty members' technological literacy, suggests
        an approach to instructional design that incorporates the possibilities of
        today's technologies, and examines how the online community offers an
        expansion of professional relationships and activities.
        ISBN: 0-7879-4280-4

TL75   Classroom Assessment and Research: An Update on Uses, Approaches,
        and Research Findings
        Thomas Angelo
        Illustrates how classroom assessment techniques (CATs) enhance both
        student learning and the scholarship of teaching. Demonstrates how CATs
        can promote good teamwork in students, help institutions answer the call
        for program accountability, and guide new teachers in developing their
        teaching philosophies.
        ISBN: 0-7879-9885-0

TL74   Changing the Way We Grade Student Performance: Classroom
        Assessment and the New Learning Paradigm
        Rebecca S. Anderson, Bruce W. Speck
        Offers alternative approaches to assessing student performance that are
        rooted in the belief that students should be active rather than passive
        learners. Explains how to use each assessment measure presented, including
        developing criteria, integrating peer and self-assessment, and assigning
        grades.
        ISBN: 0-7879-4278-2

TL73   Academic Service Learning: A Pedagogy of Action and Reflection
        Robert A. Rhoads, Jeffrey P. F. Howard
        Presents an academic conception of service learning, described as "a
        pedagogical model that intentionally integrates academic learning and
        relevant community service." Describes successful programs, and discusses
        issues that faculty and administrators must consider as they incorporate
        service learning into courses and curricula.
        ISBN: 0-7879-4276-6

TL72   Universal Challenges in Faculty Work: Fresh Perspectives from Around the World
Patricia Cranton
Educators from around the world describe issues they face in their teaching practice. National differences are put into the context of universal themes, including responding to demands for social development and reacting to influences by government policies and financial constraints.
ISBN: 0-7879-3961-7

TL71   Teaching and Learning at a Distance: What It Takes to Effectively Design, Deliver, and Evaluate Programs
Thomas E. Cyrs
Offers insights from experienced practitioners into what is needed to make teaching and learning at a distance successful for everyone involved.
ISBN: 0-7879-9884-2

TL70   Approaches to Teaching Non-Native English Speakers Across the Curriculum
David L. Sigsbee, Bruce W. Speck, Bruce Maylath
Provides strategies that help students who are non-native users of English improve their writing and speaking skills in content-area courses. Considers the points of view of the students themselves and discusses their differing levels of intent about becoming proficient in English writing and speaking.
ISBN: 0-7879-9860-5

TL69   Writing to Learn: Strategies for Assigning and Responding to Writing Across the Disciplines
Mary Deane Sorcinelli, Peter Elbow
Presents strategies and philosophies about the way writing is learned, both in the context of a discipline and as an independent skill. Focusing primarily on the best ways to give feedback about written work, the authors describe a host of alternatives that have a solid foundation in research.
ISBN: 0-7879-9859-1

TL68   Bringing Problem-Based Learning to Higher Education: Theory and Practice
LuAnn Wilkerson, Wim H. Gijselaers
Describes the basics of problem-based learning, along with the variables that affect its success. Provides examples of its application in a wide range of disciplines, including medicine, business, education, engineering, mathematics, and the sciences.
ISBN: 0-7879-9934-2

TL67   Using Active Learning in College Classes: A Range of Options for Faculty
Tracey E. Sutherland, Charles C. Bonwell
Examines the use of active learning in higher education and describes the concept of the active learning continuum, tying various practical examples of active learning to that concept.
ISBN: 0-7879-9933-4

TL66   Ethical Dimensions of College and University Teaching: Understanding and Honoring the Special Relationship Between Teachers and Students
Linc Fisch
Illustrates that responsibility to students is directly related to the understanding of one's ethical self, and that the first step in establishing that

ethical identity is self-reflection. Details the transformation of structures and attitudes that ethical teaching fosters.
ISBN: 0-7879-9910-5

TL65   Honoring Exemplary Teaching
        Marilla D. Svinicki, Robert J. Menges
        Describes programs for faculty recognition in a variety of settings and with varying purposes. Reviews research relevant to selection criteria, and offers guidelines for planning and implementing effective programs.
        ISBN: 0-7879-9979-2

TL64   Disciplinary Differences in Teaching and Learning: Implications for Practice
        Nira Hativa, Michele Marincovich
        Discusses causes and consequences of disciplinary differences in the patterns of teaching and learning; in the instructional strategies to increase teaching effectiveness; in the culture and environment in which teaching takes place; and in faculty and students' attitudes, goals, beliefs, values, philosophies, and orientations toward instruction.
        ISBN: 0-7879-9909-1

TL63   Understanding Self-Regulated Learning
        Paul R. Pintrich
        Provides a sampling of the central issues regarding self-regulated learning in college courses and classrooms, including its definition and improving students' skills in self-regulated learning.
        ISBN: 0-7879-9978-4

TL59   Collaborative Learning: Underlying Processes and Effective Techniques
        Kris Bosworth, Sharon J. Hamilton
        Provides case studies from three universities demonstrating collaborative learning in action, its potential, and its challenges. Offers guidance to faculty who wish to establish effective collaborative learning classrooms.
        ISBN: 0-7879-9998-9

TL41   Learning Communities: Creating Connections Among Students, Faculty, and Disciplines
        Faith Gabelnick, Jean MacGregor, Roberta S. Matthews, Barbara Leigh Smith
        Places learning communities within the framework of twentieth-century educational theory and reform and provides descriptions of how to design, maintain, and evaluate learning communities. Includes firsthand accounts from students and faculty in learning communities across the nation.
        ISBN: 1-55542-838-X